ARIZONA 2000

A YEARBOOK FOR THE MILLENNIUM

MARSHALL TRIMBLE

NORTHLAND
PUBLISHING

Title page: President Roosevelt at the dedication of Roosevelt Dam, 1911.

The text type was set in Adobe Garamond
The display type was set in Gill Sans and Bureau
    Gothic 17 and 79
Composed and manufactured in the United
    States of America
Designed by Trina Stahl
Edited by Kathleen Bryant
Editorial direction by Stephanie Bucholz
Production supervised by Lisa Brownfield

The use of trade names does not imply an
endorsement by the product manufacturer.

FIRST IMPRESSION
ISBN 0-87358-755-3 (hc)
ISBN 0-87358-736-7 (sc)
Library of Congress catalog card number 99-13810

Trimble , Marshall.
    Arizona 2000 : a yearbook for the millennium
    / / Marshall Trimble.
        p. cm.
    Includes bibliographical references (p.   ) and
    index.
    ISBN 0-87358-736-7 (alk. paper)
    1. Arizona–History–20th century–Miscellanea.
  I. Title. II. Title: Arizona two thousand.
  F811.A74 1999   99-13810
  979.1'03–dc21

25/500/7-99 (hc)
25/4.5M/7-99 (sc)

CONTENTS

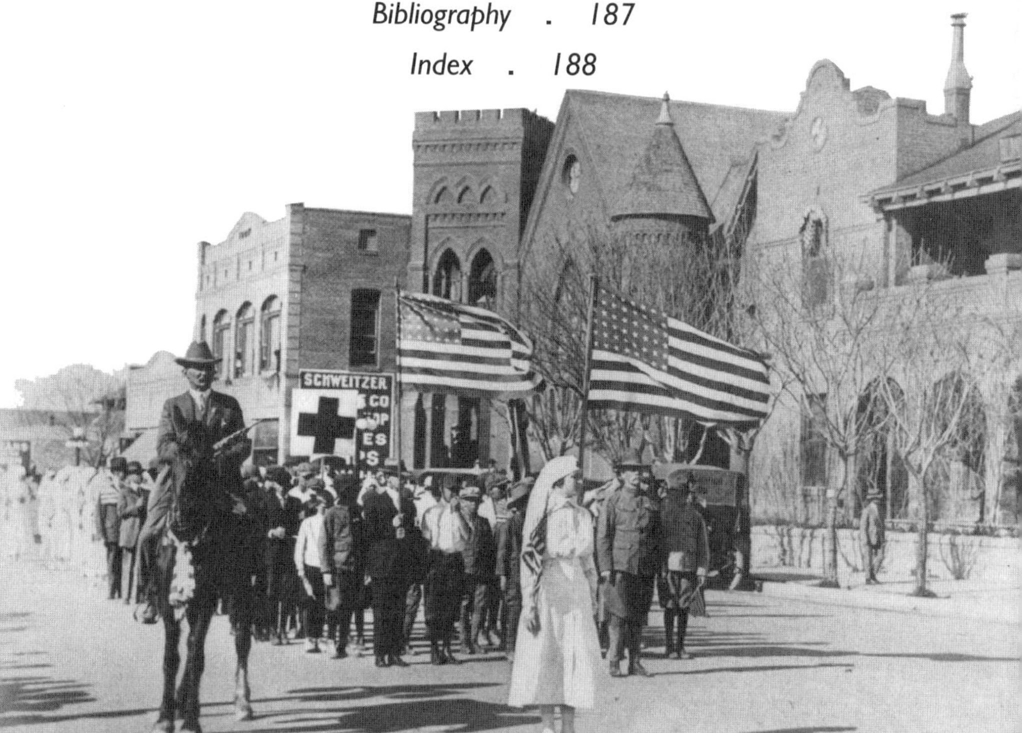

*This book is dedicated with love, pride, and respect
to my son, Cadet Roger Trimble,
United States Military Academy at West Point.*

*Class of 2001,
"'Til duty is done."*

. . .

PREFACE

Arizona historians, this writer included, have tended to focus on history prior to the twentieth century. The shoot-outs, Indian Wars, cattle ranching, railroad-building, jackass prospectors and hard-rock miners, Native Americans, conquistadors, and the rest provided enough history to fill volumes. But by the time we reach 1900, we're "plumb wore out," and the college semester is winding down, or our editors are wresting the manuscript away and rushing it off to press. At least that's how it seems. I remember, some twenty years ago, meeting in Tucson with my favorite mentor, Dr. C. Leland Sonnichsen. "Marshall," he said, "the twentieth century is where we ought to be writing. The 1930s are history now. How many times can we rewrite Wyatt Earp at the OK Corral?"

He was right, of course. Writers get comfortable in an area and tend to stay with it, especially frontier history. When Northland Publishing asked me to write a history of Arizona in the twentieth century, Doc's words of wisdom came back and I was anxious to give it a try. It turned out to be one of my most interesting projects.

I chose to break the chapters down by decades. They all had distinct personalities: The 1920s were flapper girls and sports legends; the 1930s were sobered by the Depression, and the 1940s by World War II, etc.

I have tried to draw analogies between the events in Arizona and what was going on in the rest of America. For the first half of the century this was easy: Arizona was isolated and possessed a unique character. Communication with the East was slow. The telephone and telegraph were first, then radio. Highways, where they existed, were gravel. By the

1950s all that had changed. The state was filling with newcomers and becoming more homogeneous. What was happening in Chicago and New York was also happening here. News was instantaneous.

I'll never forget hitching a ride from Ash Fork to Phoenix in the fall of 1953 to watch television for the first time. It was a World Series game between the Yankees and Dodgers. (Did anybody else ever play in the Series?) Carl Erskine struck out thirteen Yankees. I remember being awestruck, watching a game at the same time it was being played on the opposite side of the country and seeing players live instead of listening to a description by a radio announcer. Later that afternoon I walked to the local drugstore and saw the banner on the *Phoenix Gazette:* "Erskine Strikes Out Thirteen Yanks."

"I already knew that," says me.

As the century wore on, Arizona lost much of its unique character. Franchise look-alike businesses have proliferated on the landscape and there's no end in sight to the growth. And why shouldn't they come? Arizona's got great lifestyle, and it is, after all, a dry heat!

I've tried to keep the material in this book interesting and light, with a lot of popular history woven in. I couldn't resist the urge to spin a few tall tales. I've included little nuggets of information that are usually left out of traditional history books. I call them serendipitous—that's like looking for a needle in a haystack and finding the farmer's daughter instead. I hope you get the same enjoyment reading them as I did gathering them. I've also included the popular culture of the period to help provide a window into the way we were. John Steinbeck wrote, "History tells us how it was, literature tells us how it felt." To appreciate our past, we need to look at it both ways.

My career as a historian has also included being an entertainer and performer. I always try to look at the material through the eyes of my audience. Most want to sample the flavor of the times and be taken on a nostalgic trip down memory lane. That's been my purpose and I hope I've succeeded.

INTRODUCTION

Arizona is a wondrous land of spectacular color, romance, and cultural diversity. It's a wild country, shaped by the rough hand of mother nature and well-suited to the adventuresome nineteenth-century men and women who sought, as Bret Harte wrote, "a fresh deal all around."

It's a land of intimidating beauty and isolation, where reality mixes with the swirling mists of legend. In Arizona, the past isn't dead; it isn't even past.

Arizona land was once a stronghold of Native people who, for centuries, stubbornly resisted the encroachments of newcomers. Many still live on their traditional lands and practice customs and religion handed down for a thousand years.

Nearly seventy-five years before English settlers landed on the east coast of North America, Spanish explorers under the leadership of Francisco Vasquez de Coronado were crossing the rugged country of Arizona in search of the fabled Seven Cities of Gold. They would find instead a land of inhospitable deserts, searing heat, and brawny mountains so steep that a mountain goat had to "shut his eyes and walk sideways." They didn't find the riches they sought but found some good places to look. Afterward, for some forty years, questers would avoid the land some called the "northern mystery" and others referred to as a *despoblado* or badlands. Eventually, more rumors of treasure would lure the conquistadors back. This time they came to stay, settling along New Mexico's Rio Grande and southern Texas.

The origin of the name *Arizona* has been traced to a small Tohono

O'odham village or *ranchería* about twenty-five miles southwest of today's Nogales. The original name, *Ali-Shonak,* described a small spring. The rugged mountains north of the village of Ali-Shonak were the site of a fabulous silver discovery in 1736. The name Ali-Shonak didn't roll easily off the Spanish tongue and it was corrupted into *Arissona.* Word of the bonanza spread quickly and Spanish miners poured into the area to seek their fortunes. The rich native silver was described as "soft as wax." The strike became known as the *Planchas de Plata* (slabs or planks of silver.) One slab reportedly weighed more than a ton. The mining district became known as *Real de Arissona.*

Soon, thousands of prospectors were trying their hand with Lady Luck in what could be called the West's first boom town. Spanish law decreed that the royal crown was to receive a *quinto,* or 20 percent tax, on any silver found and, in an effort to thwart the unlawful pilfering, authorities tried to slap an embargo on its trade. But that didn't stop the prospectors, who cared little for bureaucrats or tax collectors. They managed to high-grade most of the silver by 1741 when, by royal order, the mines were closed. By that time, the mines had pretty much played out, but the name *Arissona* stuck.

Following the Pima Revolt of 1750, the first Spanish presidio was established along the banks of the Santa Cruz River at Tubac. With the soldiers came the first women settlers. In August 1775, Colonel Hugo O'Conor, an Irish mercenary serving in the Spanish army, established a new presidio further downstream and the modern city of Tucson was born. Settlement was slow: In 1804 there were only thirty-seven Spaniards living there.

In the mid-1770s, Spanish colonists led by Captain Juan Bautista de Anza crossed into California and settled the land from San Diego to San Francisco. Many of the first settlers in San Francisco listed their birthplace as Tubac.

During the 1780s, aggressive military campaigns led by Captain Pedro de Allande against the Apaches, combined with an appeasement policy, led to a peace agreement that lasted nearly a half-century. During that time Spanish miners and ranchers moved into southern Arizona. The missions at San Jose de Tumacacori and San Xavier del Bac were built during those tranquil times, referred to as the golden years of the Spanish period in Arizona history.

Mexican Independence came in 1821, and during the political turmoil that followed, Arizona fell into neglect. By 1835 the Apaches were back on the warpath, and with the exception of small settlements at Tucson and Tubac, Arizona was nearly deserted.

The first Americans penetrated Arizona in 1824, trapping for beaver along the rivers. Among them were such famous mountain men as Jedediah Smith, Bill Williams, Antoine Leroux, Ewing Young, "Peg Leg" Smith, and Kit Carson. By 1832 most of the beaver had been trapped out and the warrior tribes had made the place too dangerous to cross.

War broke out between the United States and Mexico in 1848, and when peace was declared two years later, Arizona lands north of the Gila River became part of the United States. Six years later the U.S. purchased the land south of the Gila to the present border with Mexico, finalizing the boundary of today's continental United States.

From 1850 until 1863 Arizona was part of New Mexico Territory. As more Americans poured into the mineral-rich country, they sought to break away from the more traditional government in Santa Fe and create a new territory, thus leading to the founding of the Arizona Territory in 1863.

Gold was discovered in Arizona's central mountains in the 1860s, manifesting the dreams of early-day Spanish conquistadors. Nineteenth-century argonauts scoured the rugged mountains and twisting canyons to pan gold from meandering streams. Rumors of vast bonanzas lured thousands of would-be millionaires to Arizona in search of riches. "If you wash your face in the Hassayampa River," someone said, "you can pan four ounces of gold dust from your whiskers." Boom towns sprang up wherever, as Mark Twain wrote, "there was a rumor and a hole in the ground." The rough-and-tumble miners gave them picturesquely whimsical names like Total Wreck, Big Bug, and Bumble Bee. Each claimed it was located on top of the mother lode and that its streets would soon be cobbled with gold nuggets. Tall tales, but they didn't thwart the true believers from selling the farm back east and heading for Arizona to try a hand with Lady Luck.

In time, the rich gold placers would play out and silver would play a big role in the future development of Arizona. Tombstone, the granddaddy of them all, was discovered in 1877, and soon became a boisterous silver town larger than San Francisco. It attracted the wide gamut of frontier society from wild women, gamblers, and gunfighters to doctors, lawyers, and mining engineers. By the time the silver mines played out in the late 1880s, America was entering the age of electricity and vast deposits of copper soon made Arizona one of the world's largest producers.

During these boisterous years Arizona gained a rather notorious reputation as "wild and woolly." The Pleasant Valley War pitted two feuding families, the Grahams and the Tewksburys, in a range war fought, in the words of Zane Grey, "to the last man." On a larger scale, Apache leaders such as Geronimo and Cochise led their braves in a courageous but futile struggle against the newcomers, who eventually overwhelmed them by sheer numbers. Geronimo and his band were the last holdouts, surrendering in 1886. Thus ended one of the longest wars in this nation's history.

Mining towns attracted a lawless, rough-hewn element. When the good citizens demanded more law and order, professional gunfighters were often hired to tame a town. Among the most famous was Wyatt Earp, who earned his reputation in the cowtowns of Kansas before coming to Tombstone to seek his fortune. Wyatt and his brothers, Virgil and Morgan, along with John Henry "Doc" Holliday, were representing the law-and-order element of Tombstone on October 26, 1881, when they took a stand against the Clantons and McLaurys at the Gunfight at OK Corral. The feud stands out today as one of the most famous gunfights in the history of the Old West.

Arriving on the bootheels of the miners were the railroads. Mules and wagons were too slow and expensive to haul the equipment in and the ore out of the rugged mountains, so track layers and gandy dancers laid in track to the mines. So many tracks led into the mountains that it looked like somebody had dumped a barrelful of black snakes over the terrain. They built railroads that couldn't be built into mountains that couldn't be climbed. The rail cars were pulled by tiny locomotives called "peanut roasters" and "coffeepots." They were so slow it was said a reasonably sober fat man could outrun one in a downhill race. But they did the job they were supposed to do. At last, the men had matched the mountains.

The Southern Pacific Railroad crossed southern Arizona in 1881. Two years later the Santa Fe finished its main line across the northern part of the territory. In 1887 a branch line from Maricopa to Phoenix was completed. Two years later that city became the permanent capital. The frontier was considered closed in 1895 when the railroad linked Phoenix with Ash Fork on the Santa Fe main line in northern Arizona. The capital city was now linked to both main lines by branch lines, but it wasn't until 1926 that the Southern Pacific finally ran a main line through Phoenix.

By the 1890s Arizonans had been clamoring for statehood for nearly two decades. For numerous reasons the politicians denied these wishes. When war with Spain came in 1898, the Arizonans, anxious to show their patriotism, were among the first to volunteer. Many were members of the legendary Rough Riders who rode to fame and glory with Teddy Roosevelt in the charge up San Juan Hill in Cuba in 1898. As the new century dawned, Arizonans looked upon the future with optimism in hopes of becoming a full partner in the union of states.

It's important that modern-day Arizonans, newcomer and native alike, share an awareness of the state's colorful history with appreciation for the past and hope for the future. The great American cowboy philosopher, Will Rogers, said it best: "The Indians never got lost because they were always looking back to see where they'd been."

A CENTURY BEGINS

"Now look, that damn cowboy is President of the United States!"

—Mark Hanna, Republican party chairman,
in 1901, referring to Vice President Teddy Roosevelt,
the irrepressible ex-Rough Rider, becoming president
following the assassination of President William McKinley

A**S A NEW CENTURY DAWNED**, Americans faced it with optimism, confidence, innocence, and some swagger. The West was "won" and the frontier was officially closed. America was looking for new frontiers to conquer. The "Splendid Little War" with Spain in 1898 had ended with the victorious United States in possession of the Philippine Islands, Guam, and Puerto Rico. Hawaii was annexed, and Wake Island was occupied. The islands of Samoa were divided between the U.S. and Germany. America had joined the exclusive club of imperialist nations of the world that included England, Italy, Russia, Germany, and France.

On September 14, 1901, President William McKinley died after being shot by an assassin a week earlier. The new president was Theodore "Teddy" Roosevelt, a soldier, statesman, author, adventurer, and advocate of the strenuous life. He was dumpy-looking physically, his eyes heavily spectacled, a toothy smile protruding from under a walrus mustache. He spoke in a high-pitched staccato, like a barking dog. He cut an almost comical figure, a caricaturist's dream. He often kept visiting dignitaries waiting while he frolicked upstairs with his six children. But there was a dynamic force in his presence: an awesome energy and ebullience. A human tornado, he loved the rough-and-tumble, swashbuckling approach to life and politics.

But beneath that floppy cowboy hat was a man possessed of keen intelligence. He consumed books at a rate of two to three a day and authored twenty-four himself. He was clearly the epitome of the zest and vigor that defined Americans during the first decade of the new century.

The Way Things Were

THE CENSUS OF 1900 reported the population of the United States at 76 million. Arizona boasted a little over 120,000 residents. Only Wyoming, Alaska, and Nevada had fewer people. Phoenix, the territorial capital, had fewer than 6,000 residents, while Tucson, Arizona's largest city, had about 7,500 residents.

Arizona's cities were becoming much like others in the nation with electricity, street cars, and theaters.

During the latter part of the nineteenth century, railroads had crisscrossed the country, laying down nearly two hundred thousand miles of track. Since the steam-driven locomotives had to take on water every forty miles or so, towns often sprang up around water tanks along the way. These forlorn burgs were generally referred to as "jerkwater," "tank," or "whistle-stop" towns.

The Cowboy President, ca. 1898.

The country was mostly rural: Nearly 60 percent of the people lived either on farms or in rural communities of fewer than 2,500 residents. But the times, they were a-changing. Factories now employed more than six million and were growing rapidly. Wages were about 10 cents an hour for a six-day work week. Workers earned some $12 a week. A factory worker earned only about $500 a year, and children labored for as little as 25 cents a day. The work day had decreased from twelve hours to ten, and for many, Saturday was becoming a half-holiday. The annual income per capita in 1870 was $779. By 1900, it had risen to $1,164.

Prices were relatively low. Eggs sold for 12 cents a dozen; sirloin steak sold for 24 cents a pound. A man's expensive suit cost around $9, and a cheaper one sold for around $3.75. A pair of Levi's cost 75 cents. Trousers went for $1.25, as did a pair of shoes. A man's shirt cost 50 cents. Women's apparel, then as now, was more expensive.

Drugstores had something for everybody. A glass of Coca-Cola sold for a nickel. One could purchase Heidi's candy with licorice and mints for 5 cents a box. And a set of false teeth sold for $5.

Meanwhile, in Wild and Woolly Arizona

A NEW CENTURY WAS BORN and an old one had died. But out in Arizona it was still the Old West, and it was still wild and woolly. On February 15, 1900, at the train station in Fairbank, located on the San Pedro River in Cochise County, five men made a daring attempt to rob the train. The outlaws waited at the station, acting like drunk and rowdy cowboys to deceive the locals. As the train slowly pulled into the station, they suddenly sobered up, drew their six-guns, and opened fire on the shotgun messenger standing in the open doorway of the Wells Fargo car.

The desperadoes planned well but didn't reckon on the shotgun messenger's being the famed ex–Texas Ranger Jeff Milton, who was now working for Wells Fargo. Their barrage seriously wounded Milton, who fell backwards, dropping out of sight behind a large baggage trunk. As they charged the express car, he rose up with a sawed-off ten-gauge shotgun and cut down the lead man, Three-Finger Jack Dunlap. Bravo Juan Yoas, who was right behind, spun around when he saw Milton's shotgun and caught a load of buckshot in the seat of his pants.

The luckless outlaws gathered their wounded and rode away without the loot. Three-Finger Jack Dunlap, mortally wounded, was left along the trail by his fair-weather friends.

In Fairbank, a posse was organized and went in hot pursuit. A few miles down the trail they came upon Three-Finger Jack. He was displeased that his companions left him behind, so in a dying confession, he fingered his cohorts. He also identified the gang's organizers as

Willcox constable Burt Alvord and his deputies, Billy Stiles and Bill Downing. A few months earlier that trio had robbed another train outside Willcox. Investigators were suspicious but had no proof. After Three-Finger Jack's confession, the gang was rounded up and hauled off to the county jail at Tombstone.

Jeff Milton survived his wounds and died in Tucson in 1948 with his boots off.

In another round of violence, on July 16, 1900, Warren Earp, the youngest of the famous Earp brothers, was gunned down in a Willcox saloon.

Pearl Hart, the "Girl Bandit."

Also in 1900, Pearl Hart, the famed "Girl Bandit," was sentenced to five years in prison for her part in a stagecoach robbery the year before. At her first trial, pretty Pearl was an unabashed flirt, revealing her shapely ankles and coquettish smile to an all-male jury. These red-blooded males found Pearl innocent but declared her cohort, Joe Boot, guilty as charged. The outraged judge ordered her tried again on another charge, that of interfering with the U.S. Mail (Male?). A sympathetic Eastern press condemned callous Arizonans for sending such a fine specimen of Eve's flesh as Pearl to that dastardly prison in Yuma. She was released from prison after faking a pregnancy and went on the lecture circuit for a brief time, explaining to audiences she'd robbed the stage to get money to visit her sick mother in the East. Pearl's escapade turned out to be the last stagecoach robbery in America.

A demure Pearl dolled up for trial.

Writing the West

MANY WRITERS OF WESTERN FICTION found their way into Arizona, searching for settings for their stories. The most famous was Zane Grey, who first came to Arizona in 1907. Born Pearl Zane Grey, he was trained as a dentist, but chose to become a writer instead. On his first Arizona visit, he explored much of the land north of the Grand Canyon on horseback. That resulted in a nonfiction work, *The Last of the Plainsmen,* which presented a striking picture of the Arizona Strip and North Rim. That area would also become the setting for one of his most famous novels, *Riders of the Purple Sage,* in 1912. It was his first major success and was followed by more than eighty books.

In 1918 he visited the Tonto Basin area at the foot of the Mogollon Rim and eventually built a lodge there. He came back each year until 1929 to hunt with his old friend and guide "Babe" Haught. His experiences in the basin gained him knowledge of the famous Pleasant Valley War and inspired his novel on the feud between the Grahams and Tewksburys, *To the Last Man.*

Like many popular writers, Grey was criticized by literary scholars, yet his books and his following remain strong to this day. He did as much as any writer to popularize the myth of the cowboy.

Keeping the West in Food and Wives

FRED HARVEY WAS A TRAVELING SALESMAN who'd had some horrible experiences at eating establishments while traveling by rail. The English gentleman approached the Santa Fe Railroad with the novel idea of providing passengers with attractive surroundings, superior service, and above all, good food. The company accepted his proposal enthusiastically, for food service had been one of the most serious problems plaguing railroads at the time. The Santa Fe agreed to supply the buildings and transport food, furnishings, and personnel, all free of charge. In addition, the shrewd entrepreneur Harvey was to receive all the profits from this venture.

THE GRAND CANYON LINE

☀ Until 1901 the only way to transport tourists to the Grand Canyon was by stagecoach. For $20 one could "enjoy" a dusty, eleven-hour, bone-jarring trip some seventy miles from Flagstaff. That year the Santa Fe completed the sixty-four-mile rail line from Williams, and for just $3.95, one could now reach the Canyon comfortably by rail. Over the next sixty-seven years such dignitaries as presidents Theodore Roosevelt, William Howard Taft, Franklin D. Roosevelt, and Dwight D. Eisenhower, as well as such celebrities as Clark Gable, Edgar Bergen, Jimmy Durante, and Doris Day traveled the Grand Canyon Line.

America's love affair with the railroads dwindled as the automobile became popular, and in 1968 the Santa Fe closed the Grand Canyon line. But in 1989 the Grand Canyon Railroad was reborn, and once again tourists would take the nostalgic ride from Williams in vintage cars pulled by a 1910 steam locomotive.

The first Harvey House opened in Topeka, Kansas, in 1876 and was a resounding success. Over the next twenty years Harvey opened his Spanish-style restaurants and hotels along the Santa Fe main line. The early ones were spaced about a hundred miles apart to (as one said), "keep western traffic from settling in one place where Harvey served his meals."

Arizona had five Harvey Houses along the main line in the early days. These were located in Winslow, Williams, Ash Fork, Seligman, and Kingman. French chefs were hired away from prominent eastern restaurants and paid high wages. Young women were hired as waitresses and dubbed "Harvey Girls." Humorist Will Rogers quipped, "Fred Harvey kept the West supplied in food and wives."

In 1905 the Fred Harvey Company opened the world's "grandest" hotel, El Tovar, perched precariously on the South Rim of the Grand Canyon. The long, rambling inn, built with massive Kaibab limestone blocks and durable split logs from Oregon, was originally a playground for the rich during those days when only the affluent could afford to travel. The architectural design is a blend of Swiss chalet and Scandinavian hunting lodge, and the construction work was done by Hopis. The spacious lobby was a social gathering place for kings, queens, and presidents. Despite the presence of high society, the prices were reasonable. A room with a bath went for six to eight dollars. Breakfast and lunch cost a dollar, and a full-course dinner served by one of the famous Harvey Girls was a dollar and a half. In all aspects, the hotel epitomized Fred Harvey elegance.

Horseless Carriages

IT HAD BEEN TWO GENERATIONS since America had seen a major war. The business of the country was peace and prosperity, but the average worker earned only 22 cents an hour. Automobiles sold for about $1,550. Trucks and busses hadn't been invented yet and there were less than 150 miles of paved roads in the entire United States.

When Arizona became a state in 1912, there were fewer than 2,000 vehicles in the entire state. Gasoline and oil were sold in drugstores, mechanical work was done at the blacksmith shop, and livery stables became garages. Who would have prophesied that these spindly, fragile gas buggies, sold as a sideline in bicycle shops and wagon yards, would soon make up the nation's largest manufacturing industry?

Some women were bold enough to flout social taboos and customs of the day. A popular fad was getting the body tattooed. Jenny Jerome, the mother of Sir Winston Churchill, had a tattoo of a snake curled around her wrist. The legendary mining town of Jerome was named for Jenny's cousin Eugene, a New York banker.

In with the New

IT WAS THE DAWNING of the age of electricity. Thomas Edison's Moving Picture Machine, in a 1895 ad, promoted "life-size motion pictures." The Edison Kinetoscope flipped 46 pictures a second or 2,760 a minute, claiming "each picture has a slight change of motion, creat[ing] an illusion of movable figures." Typewriters and sewing machines were becoming more common.

The monetary debate was revived in 1900 with the adoption of the

Gold Standard Act. This act declared that the gold dollar was the sole monetary standard of currency. The Republicans favored the gold standard and were opposed adamantly by free silver states such as Arizona. It was said at the time that anyone in Arizona who admitted to being a Republican was either a damn fool or a newcomer.

Jackass prospectors scoured the West for new bonanzas. Gold was discovered in 1902 around what became known as Oatman. The area produced more than two million ounces of the yellow metal, worth $42 million, making it Arizona's greatest predominately gold-mining area. Most of that was produced when the price of gold was $20 an ounce. At today's prices the sum would be considerably more.

On February 24, 1901, the new capitol building on west Washington Street was dedicated by Governor Nathan Oakes Murphy. (Phoenix had been awarded the territorial capital in 1889, after the so-called "capital on wheels" had moved from Prescott to Tucson and back to Prescott again by the horse-trading territorial assembly.)

The Arizona Rangers

IN JANUARY OF 1901, Governor Murphy was given authorization to form a small, mobile company of Arizona Rangers. There was a great need for an independent force of lawmen. Large gangs of cattle rustlers still roamed the mountains of eastern Arizona and along the Mexican border. The company was eventually expanded to number twenty-six men.

A rough-and-tumble and proud breed, they wore no uniforms, dressing instead like cowboys. They kept their badges concealed and infiltrated the rustler gangs that terrorized southeastern Arizona. When a Ranger had the goods on the rustlers, he boldly pinned on his badge and made the arrest. It took a lot of sand to be an Arizona Ranger.

The role of the Arizona Rangers shifted from running down cattle rustlers to squelching striking copper miners. The legislature had passed a law cutting the work day from ten hours to eight with no cut in pay. One mining company responded by cutting the work shift but paying for only nine hours of work, resulting in a drop in pay. On June 6, 1903,

Arizona Ranger W. K. Farnsworth holding his trusty 1895 Winchester .30–.40.

the Rangers were called upon to help put down a riot of striking hard-rock miners in Morenci. Three days later, in a torrential downpour, some two thousand angry miners armed themselves and prepared to make a fight of it. The miners shut down the entire mining district by blocking tunnels and preventing ore from being loaded onto railroad cars. It was the largest strike in Arizona history prior to World War I.

A coalition between law enforcement and mine owners, combined with the elements, defeated the strikers. The summer monsoons arrived early that year and torrential rains in the high country sent raging waters cascading down Chase Creek and the San Francisco River. Homes and businesses were caught up in the floodwaters and swept away. The strikers quickly lost interest in the labor cause as they began to search the muddy waters for loved ones lost in the flood. Some fifty people died, and when federal troops arrived, the miners meekly surrendered their weapons. The leaders were arrested and eventually sent to the territorial prison at Yuma. The leaders, including "Three Finger" Jack Laustaunau, an agitator sent out from Chicago by an anarchist labor organization, was convicted of inciting miners to riot. While in prison, this professional troublemaker became one of Yuma's most incorrigible inmates, organizing prisoner work strikes and presenting outrageous demands.

The strike is perhaps best remembered today for the famous photograph taken of the Arizona Rangers lined up with their trusty Winchesters.

Despite the Rangers' popularity, the legislature voted them out of existence in 1909. Politics played a large role in the Rangers' demise. Counties not affected by outlawry didn't want to ante up to support a territorial-wide police force.

Headlines, 1903

ON FEBRUARY 4, 1903, the Salt River Water Users Association, the fore-runner to the Salt River Project, was organized. As a result of the 1902 Newlands or Reclamation Act, Tonto Dam (eventually renamed Theodore Roosevelt Dam) was constructed on the Salt River to insure a

THE MYTH OF THE WEST

In 1903 Edwin S. Porter made the first motion picture, The Great Train Robbery, *a twelve-minute Western filmed in the wilds of New Jersey. The movie capped off its action with a gunshot fired directly at the audience. Western movies soon became the rage and Arizona would become one of the most popular locations. The Old West was rapidly fading from reality into the realm of mythology. A year earlier Owen Wister had written the Western classic,* The Virginian. *That book, along with dime novels, movies, and Buffalo Bill's Wild West Show, were major contributors in creating the myth of the cowboy and the American West that still thrives in the hearts and minds of people all over the world.*

reliable supply of water and guarantee future settlement in the Salt River Valley. Farmers put up their lands as collateral to pay for the dam. The debt wasn't paid in full until 1955.

A Pioneer in Flight

THE AGE OF FLIGHT began on December 17, 1903, at Kitty Hawk, North Carolina, when Orville Wright went aloft for 59 seconds in a "whopper flying machine" for a distance of 852 feet.

Arizona's first flight took place on February 12, 1910, when Charles Hamilton, billing himself as the "Man-Bird," flew his bamboo-and-silk airplane in a race against a Studebaker car at the state fairgrounds. The race covered five miles and wound up in a draw, as each entrant won on successive days. Hamilton hauled the ship to Tucson, where he was paid $2,000 to dazzle the audience with a flight of forty miles per hour, soaring to an altitude of nine hundred feet. The citizens of Patagonia offered him twice that amount to perform in their town, but Hamilton passed on the offer and headed on to El Paso.

In 1915 Katherine Stinson, a pretty, nineteen-year-old aviatrix, thrilled Tucsonians with a series of loop-the-loops and the terrifying death-dip. On November 5, she was given the honor of delivering the first "official" air mail in Arizona. She flew a mail sack from the fairgrounds in Tucson to the local post office and dropped it in a nearby vacant lot. Four years later Tucson opened the nation's first municipal airport.

A New Look at the Old Ones

DURING THE LATTER PART of the nineteenth century and early part of the twentieth, archaeologists, professional and amateur, studied places like Canyon de Chelly, near Chinle; Wupatki, near Flagstaff; Montezuma's Castle, in the Verde Valley; Betatakin and Keet Seel, near Kayenta; Tonto Ruins, along the Salt River; and Casa Grande, along the Gila River.

From the work of these pioneer archaeologists and those that followed we now know that about four thousand years ago corn, or maize, was introduced from Mexico. For the first time, Arizona's early inhabitants could grow crops. Over the centuries, as they depended more on agriculture and less on wild plants, they began to build permanent dwellings.

Arizona's prehistoric cultures (Anasazi, Hohokam, Sinagua, Mogollon, Patayan, and Salado) rose, evolved, thrived, and declined roughly between the time of Christ and A.D. 1400, then mysteriously "went away." In many instances, they left their dwellings intact, as if they'd just gone off on vacation.

Dating these fabulous sites was made possible through techniques developed by archaeologists and other scientists. One of the most accurate was dendrochronology, or tree-ring dating, developed in Arizona by Dr. Andrew E. Douglass. He was in the Flagstaff area in the early 1900s when he noticed that certain kinds of living trees, such as the ponderosa pine, have growth rings of varying widths, depending on the amount of annual rainfall. Dr. Douglass compiled a master time chart of tree-ring data dating back thousands of years, to the time of Babylon. By comparing core samples from beams of ancient dwellings to the master time chart, he could determine the year those beams were cut by ancient peoples. (Today it's possible to see a giant storytelling cross section or "slice of history" at the Arizona State Museum on the University of Arizona campus in Tucson.)

Thanks to the work of Dr. Douglass we know, for example, that Sunset Crater was formed in the years 1064 and 1065, burying prehistoric dwellings and driving their builders away. We also know the builders returned to farm the land "mulched" by volcanic cinders.

Because of the value of the artifacts found around ancient sites, illegal pot hunters have been the scourge of the Southwest for decades. Any disturbance puts the whole site out of context, and the credibility of later scientific study is lost. To discourage pot hunters, the National Antiquities Act of 1906 was passed, providing fines for disturbing sites on federal, Indian, and state lands. The act also gave the president the power to designate national monuments. As a result, Arizona gained several monuments in the century's first two decades, including Montezuma Castle, Tonto National Forest, Keet Seel and Betatakin (Cave Pueblos of the Navajo National Monument), Walnut Canyon, Casa Grande, and Grand Canyon National Park.

A New Star in the Flag

SINCE THE 1870s, territorial residents had been clamoring for statehood. A resolution was introduced in 1892 but went nowhere. When war was declared on Spain and the country began to mobilize, young Arizonans had eagerly volunteered to join the fight in hopes of convincing Congress they were qualified to join the union of states. During the war in Cuba, just prior to the charge up San Juan Hill, Rough Rider Captain Buckey O'Neill declared, "Who would not risk his life for a new star in the flag?" On July 1, 1898, a sniper's fatal bullet drove the gallant Irishman to the ground, and by the turn of the century Arizonans felt they had paid their dues.

The boys had come home from the war in 1898 with high hopes a grateful nation would bestow statehood on their territory, but it would be another fourteen years of anxious waiting. The real reason for the delay was that the Republican-dominated Congress resisted adding two more Democrats to the Senate, not to mention the gradual shift of power from east to west that continues to this day.

Members of Congress offered several reasons to delay statehood for Arizona, including the free silver issue, a lack of decent roads, the Apache wars, the Pleasant Valley War, and the Cochise County feud (highlighted by the so-called "Gunfight at the OK Corral"). All had combined to create the illusion of a wild and woolly place populated with nothing but Apaches, outlaws, rattlesnakes, cactus, and Democrats.

Powerful mining interests and railroads opposed statehood early because of the lucrative land grants, odd-numbered sections of land for twenty miles on each side of the tracks given to railroads during territorial days as incentive to build the land. The railroads, in turn, sold the land to ranchers. Later, they favored it, believing they could control taxation issues more easily on a state government rather than federal government level.

On May 8, 1900, President William McKinley spent the day in Phoenix and made a whistle-stop in Tucson without once mentioning statehood. Senator Albert Beverage of Indiana, Chairman of the Committee on Territories, visited Arizona briefly and declared it a bleak desert. Bills proposing statehood withered and died in committees. Senator Thomas Bard of California arrogantly claimed Arizonans weren't intelligent enough to have statehood. He also thought the territory had too many Mormons and Indians. Another senator who opposed statehood was Knute Nelson of Minnesota. He addressed the un-American area by saying in a thick Norwegian accent, "Ay tank dose fellairs en Arizona not beene goot enofe Americaines. To bay goot seetyzain, a fellair moost bay Ameracaine."

In 1902 Senator Beverage and his friends tried to combine Arizona and New Mexico into one state to be called "Montezuma." To placate

Phoenix, 1900. Camelback Mountain is in the background. In the center of the picture is the fabulous Adams Hotel. Built in 1895, it burned in 1910 in what is still the most spectacular fire in Phoenix history.

the irate Arizonans, they changed the name to Arizona but located the capital in Santa Fe. The joint statehood bill passed the House in 1904. President Roosevelt favored it, causing Arizonans to seethe. Mass town meetings were held all over the territory in protest. Indignant Phoenicians threatened to change the name of Roosevelt Street to Cleveland.

Arizona's territorial delegate, the venerable Mark Smith, a former Tombstone lawyer, cleverly attached an amendment to the Foraker Amendment that required both territories to approve. The New Mexicans favored it two-to-one, but the stubborn Arizonans over-whelmingly opposed the measure by 16,265 to 3,141 votes, so it was back to the drawing board.

Headlines, 1904-1908

THE WINTER OF 1904–05 was a wet one in Arizona. One newspaper reported, "The rains which are so copious are doing double duty in Arizona, insuring good crops, and at the same time keeping many of the legislators at home, thus preventing them from doing much damage in law making."

In January 1906, Flagstaff was rocked by a series of earthquakes, a precursor, perhaps, to the great earthquake that destroyed the city of San Francisco a few months later.

On June 1, the mule-drawn street car made its last run in Tucson. It was replaced by the newfangled electric car.

In 1907 the territorial legislature passed a law prohibiting women from entering saloons in Arizona.

In 1908 the city of Tucson passed an ordinance prohibiting spitting on the sidewalk. A year later citizens of Prescott declared they were putting an end to smoking by students.

On January 1, 1908, the era of all-night saloons ended in Tucson when the city council determined they must close at midnight. Saloon-keepers retaliated by raising the price of a glass of beer to ten cents.

That same year Wilbur and Orville Wright began providing airplanes for the army that remained aloft for an hour and flew at a speed of forty miles per hour.

As the Decade Closed

BY 1909 there were ten thousand movie theaters in the United States. A ticket cost a dime, and Mary Pickford was earning forty dollars a week making pictures.

In 1909 the great Chiricahua Apache leader Geronimo died at the age of eighty. That same year Pima County dropped murder charges against the wily warrior that had been on the books since 1886.

Also in 1909, the great artist Frederic Remington died of acute appendicitis at the age of forty-eight. He began his career in the 1880s, coming to Arizona to illustrate the Geronimo Campaign for *Harper's Weekly.*

Perhaps the most significant Arizona event of 1909 occurred on New Year's Day. On that day Baron and Josephine Goldwater became the proud parents of a new baby, who was given the name Barry. With the exception of his mother, little did anyone realize that this energetic infant would grow up to become one of the most important figures in not only Arizona's history, but America's and the world's as well. Statesman, civic reformer, philanthropist, adventurer, writer, photographer, military pilot—Barry Goldwater was a true renaissance man. Born with the new century, he would die with the old on May 29, 1998.

THE TEENS

*"If Phoenix continues to grow
at this rapid rate, by the year 2000,
the population will reach 100,000."*

—A prophetic banker in a 1912 speech

O N THE EVENING OF MAY 11, 1910, the Phoenix and Eastern Railroad train pulled out of Phoenix and chuffed its way southward across the desert to where the branch line joined the Southern Pacific main line at Maricopa. On board, the Woodson brothers, Ernie and Oscar (later referred to in the press as the "beardless boy bandits"), sat nervously in their seats.

As the train approached the spot where they had earlier tied rented horses, they brandished their six-guns and made the conductor stop. Then they pilfered some three hundred dollars from the pockets of the passengers, mounted their horses, and headed across the hot desert for the Mexican border.

When word of the robbery reached Phoenix, Maricopa County Sheriff Carl Hayden loaded a posse on a special train, put their horses in cattle cars, and headed for the site of the robbery. Using Pima Indian trackers the posse easily picked up the trail. Hayden meanwhile headed on to Maricopa, where he enlisted the services of a local hotel owner, J. F. McCarthy, and his powerful $3,000 Dayton-Stoddard touring automobile. It was the first time in American history a posse used the horseless carriage to pursue desperadoes.

At the small Indian community of Cuckelbur, the posse picked up the bandits' trail and sped across cactus patches and arroyos in hot pursuit. The Woodsons, unaware of the posse on their trail, had stopped to rest under a large palo verde tree. By now the desert heat had taken its toll on their horses. Believing the approaching automobile to be miners out inspecting their claims, they rushed out, waving their arms.

Ernie and Oscar got a big surprise when several officers jumped out of the car with guns drawn. Looking down the barrels of several rifles,

Ernie dropped his six-gun and meekly surrendered. Oscar wasn't ready to give up yet. His hand dipped in his pocket, fingering the rented revolver. "Throw down your gun or I'll shoot," one of the deputies shouted.

Sheriff Hayden, pistol in hand, told the officer to stand easy. The sheriff then calmly walked toward the youngster and in a steady voice told him to give up. After a long pause the boy relented. The Woodsons were then shackled and hauled off to Phoenix. Hayden's bravery was accentuated by the fact that his own revolver was unloaded when he walked up to the outlaws and ordered them to surrender.

Carl Hayden's fame as a cool and steady lawman in the line of fire spread far and wide. Two years later, when Arizona achieved statehood, Hayden threw his hat in the ring, running for the single House seat. The recognition he'd received for his capture of the Woodson brothers played a large part in his being elected to Congress. In 1926 he ran for the Senate and remained there until 1969. When he retired, Hayden was one of the most powerful politicians in Washington. His lifetime spanned a period in history that ranged from the Gunfight at the OK Corral to Neil Armstrong's walk on the moon. *Time* magazine once referred to him as the "last link between the New Frontier and the real one."

A Brief Flame

MOST PEOPLE KNOW that on April 16, 1912, the *Titanic* struck an iceberg and sunk in the Atlantic with more than fifteen hundred people aboard. Few recall that on that same day, "Flame" Delhi became Arizona's first major league baseball player.

Delhi, the son of a gold miner, was born at Harqua Hala, south of present-day Salome. Christened Lee William Delhi, he became better known as Flame when he was pitching in the Pacific Coast League in 1910 and a sports writer nicknamed him for his blazing fastball. Flame Delhi was considered the best pitcher in the league, and the majors held a bidding war for his services the following season. The Chicago White Sox outbid the Cincinnati Reds and purchased his contract for $5,000. He reported for spring training in February 1912, the same month Arizona gained statehood.

The rest of the story has an ironic twist. Delhi came back to Arizona and pitched for Ray Mines. In exchange for his services, the company trained him as a mining engineer. During the Great Depression of the 1930s, Flame Delhi was earning $80,000 a year, the same salary as baseball's greatest player, Babe Ruth.

The Saga of Statehood Continues

THE QUEST FOR STATEHOOD was finally reaching its successful end. On June 20, 1910, President William Howard Taft signed the Arizona statehood bill, better known as the Enabling Act. It provided for a constitutional convention, and delegates were chosen in county party conventions. Democrat George W. P. Hunt of Globe was elected president of the convention and Morris Goldwater of Prescott, vice president. Delegates were paid four dollars a day, while clerks and other staff were paid a dollar more.

The Democrats and their progressive platform prevailed, winning forty-one seats. This was a time when people were demanding a bigger voice in government. Among the demands were elections by direct primary and the controversial initiative, referendum, and recall.

Conservative delegates argued that President Taft, a former judge, would surely veto the constitution if the provision for the recall of judges was passed. On the other hand, labor unions wanted it as leverage against judges who, at the behest of powerful copper companies, issued injunctions against striking workers. All three measures—initiative, referendum, and recall—were approved. In addition, the delegates voted not to make segregation of schools compulsory. Two other popular reforms of the day, women's suffrage and prohibition, were defeated. Women's suffrage lost despite a postcard that depicted a drunk and a young mother. The caption: "This man can vote. This woman cannot."

Because of their long dislike for Washington-appointed governors, the delegates severely limited the appointive power of the chief executive. Top political offices in the state would be elected and independent of the governor. (This would curtail the power of the governor until the 1960s, when the executive branch was streamlined into "super departments," which were headed by a director appointed by the governor.)

The constitutional convention wrapped up on December 9, and all but three delegates signed. A few weeks later the voters approved it by a margin of 12,584 to 3,920. The joint Congressional resolution providing for statehood was vetoed by President Taft.

In Arizona, cooler heads prevailed, and the recall was removed. Another election was held on December 12, 1911, and the vote was 14,963 in favor and 1,980 against removing the recall, smoothing the way to statehood. (On November 5, 1912, the recall was reinserted, and in that same election the Arizonans vented their anger on "Billy" Taft. He finished fourth in a field of four behind Woodrow Wilson, Teddy Roosevelt, and Eugene V. Debs.)

The voters in that 1911 election chose George W. P. Hunt as their first governor, Marcus Aurelius Smith and Henry F. Ashurst as their two U.S. Senators, and Carl Hayden as Congressman. (Statehood was inevitable at this point, and elections were held so the politicians would "hit the ground running.")

Hunt, a consummate politician, would be elected to two-year terms

George Willey Paul Hunt's nicknames included
"Old Walrus" and "King George VII" (for his seven terms).

seven times, causing his opponents to refer to him as "George the Seventh" and humorist Will Rogers to dub him "Arizona's perennial governor." He loved to campaign. He knew how to charm the voters, too. He used to buy cases of preserves at the grocery store, boil the labels off, then greet some local official's wife by saying, "My wife cooked up these preserves and she'd like for you to have a jar." Needless to say, he always made a favorable impression with these tactics.

Mark Smith was a colorful former Tombstone lawyer and territorial delegate to Washington. Ashurst was an ex-cattle rancher. Earlier, on June 2, 1911, Ashurst met his Republican opponent, M. G. Burns, in Prescott, where a fist fight ensued. Ashurst won the fight and the election.

Hayden, a quiet man, became known as a political "workhorse," while Ashurst was the opposite—a genuine "show horse." He loved to quote Shakespeare and was a gifted and colorful elocutionist. In Washington he was known as the "Silver-Tongued Orator of the Colorado," or more succinctly, "Five-Syllable Henry."

The Greatest Day in Arizona History

STATEHOOD AT LONG LAST ARRIVED on February 14, 1912, when Taft signed the proclamation. The news set off widespread celebration among Arizonans, who cast off the chains of second-class territorial status. In Prescott, a "statehood tree" was planted in the courthouse plaza. The University of Arizona in Tucson dismissed all 254 students from classes. Boisterous Bisbee miners set off dynamite, nearly blowing off the top of Copper Queen Mountain, and Snowflake locals celebrated by blowing up an anvil. In Phoenix, whistles started blowing and people took to the streets, firing pistols into the air. The marriage of Joe Melczer and Hazel Goldberg had been delayed that morning so they could be the first couple married in the new state of Arizona. When the news arrived, vows were exchanged, and the rings were presented by a fidgety three-year-old ring bearer named Barry Goldwater.

At 11:15 A.M. the portly Governor Hunt left the Ford Hotel in downtown Phoenix and took the forty-five-minute walk down Washington Street to the capitol, crossing irrigation ditches and dodging potholes and horse manure along the way. He wanted to set a good example of thrift but quickly lost his enthusiasm. From then on he rode in a chauffeur-driven $3,000 limousine that cost taxpayers $300 a month to maintain.

At the capitol, silver-tongued orator and perennial presidential candidate William Jennings Bryan spoke without a microphone for two hours nonstop to a crowd of five thousand. A forty-eight-round cannon salute was intended but was halted ten rounds short when windows in the capitol began to shatter and horses started bucking their riders.

At the close of the greatest day in Arizona history, it was reported by one newspaper that in spite of all the festivities, only a handful of people spent the night in jail.

Sporting News

IN THE WORLD OF SPORTS during the decade Lewis Tewanima, the great Hopi distance runner from Second Mesa, won the Silver Medal in the ten-thousand-meter run during the 1912 Olympics at Stockholm. (In the 1908 Olympics at London, he'd finished ninth in the marathon.) The "Happy Hopi from Shongopovi" trained by chasing jackrabbits and running sixty-seven miles to Winslow and back, all in the same day. Tewanima and the legendary Sac Fox Indian from Oklahoma, Jim Thorpe, comprised the nucleus of the Carlisle Indian School track team coached by Pop Warner.

The War Next Door

DURING THE MEXICAN WAR, 1846–48, the new republic had lost half of its land to the Americans, and by 1910 Mexico was a political powder keg, ready to explode. For decades foreign investors had exploited her natural resources. American capitalists alone had invested billions of dollars in railroads, oil, and mining. Fifty thousand Americans had taken residency in Mexico. The Hearst family owned a ranch the size of Rhode Island. A small group of wealthy Mexican landowners and foreign investors controlled all the wealth, while the great majority of her fifteen million citizens were landless and poor.

Mexico was the most-policed country in the world, ruled by martial law, without courts and with the *Rurales,* who loved to shoot. Citizens lived in terror.

The revolution began in 1910, and a year later the despotic dictator, Porfirio Diaz, dictatorial president of Mexico from 1876 to 1911, was driven from office. He was replaced by a California-educated visionary named Francisco Madero, who was unable to control the pernicious forces within the revolution. Madero was murdered in 1913 and replaced by General Victoriano Huerta, a full-blooded Aztec who was part of the clique that murdered Madero.

The ascendancy of Huerta caught the ire of President Woodrow Wilson. The president, a former teacher, decided to "teach the South American republics how to elect good men." He allowed the free flow of arms into Mexico to supply the followers of Francisco "Pancho" Villa and Venustiano Carranza.

American adventurers, especially barnstorming pilots, were in demand by both sides. Aerial combat was in its embryonic state. In early May 1913, Charlie Ford of Douglas flew his homemade plane across the border at Agua Prieta and dropped his homemade bombs on a railroad trestle. This is considered the first aggressive aerial bombing attack in the Western Hemisphere.

Mexican rebels enlisted American Didier Masson to smuggle a biplane across the border near Nogales. His first combat mission took place on May 10, 1913, when he attacked a *federale* gunboat lying offshore near Guaymas. Masson circled the gunboat at five thousand feet while his assistant, Gustavo Camina, hurled homemade bombs, foot-long pipes filled with dynamite, at the enemy below. The bombs missed their target but did manage to convince the crew to jump overboard and swim for shore.

General Francisco "Pancho" Villa,
ca. 1915.

Villa hired a flyer named Dean Lamb, and the *federales* employed Phil Roder. Most of the time the flimsy biplanes swooped over trenches and tossed out homemade pipe bombs on the hapless ground troops. The planes had no guns, so when they met in the skies, the pilots fought it out with six-shooters.

Citizens of communities like Bisbee and Douglas had ringside seats to the battles at Naco and Agua Prieta. The opposing forces did all they could to avoid firing toward the American side of the border, but occasionally a stray bullet would send the spectators scurrying for cover. One lady reported that a bullet came through her window and clipped the tail feathers off her pet parakeet. Another witness reported that the Mexicans had experimented with a cannon attached to the back of a horse. The recoil of the gun caused the horse to do a double back flip and the project was abandoned.

During one battle at Naco, Sonora, Cochise County Sheriff Harry Wheeler rode out between the opposing armies with a white flag and requested they change positions, as their bullets were flying into the sister city of Naco, Arizona. The two generals acquiesced and moved their armies.

Pancho Villa was not only an unconventional military strategist; he had a flair for showmanship as well. He found a way to commercialize war by selling the motion picture rights to the revolution to the Mutual Film Corporation, which followed the action with Villa's troops. The accommodating Villa even agreed to stage his battles when the light was right for filming. Ironically, *The Life of Villa* was a box-office flop because audiences didn't believe the movie was realistic enough.

Mexico couldn't agree on who should run the government. Pancho Villa was a power in the north, and Emiliano Zapata was a force in the south. Neither was political enough to run a government, so President Wilson threw his support to Carranza. This action infuriated Villa, and on March 9, 1916, a band of *Villistas* crossed the border and attacked the little town of Columbus, New Mexico. They hit the military post and caught U.S. troops by surprise. The U.S. forces quickly recovered and drove the rebels back across the border. The action left seventeen Americans and sixty-seven *Villistas* dead.

THE PUNITIVE EXPEDITION

✴ *Villa's raid on Columbus, New Mexico, caused President Wilson to send a Punitive Expedition into Mexico to capture and punish Villa. The expedition, led by General John J. "Black Jack" Pershing, plunged five hundred miles into Mexico and pursued the elusive Villa unsuccessfully for a nearly a year.*

Pershing's aide-de-camp during the campaign was a tough, dashing young lieutenant named George Smith Patton, Jr. His reputation as a warrior extraordinaire *began on the campaign when he gunned down two* Villista *soldiers with his six-shooter.*

Major George Langhorne, a dapper, well-to-do career officer brought along his chauffeur-driven, eight-cylinder Cadillac. He rode in high style while leading his men on a chase against the Villista *raiders. At one point in the pursuit the car "bounded over ditches and bushes like a steeplechaser." The only noticeable damage was a wounded suspension system.*

Cleverly avoiding capture by the Americans, the elusive Villa became a folk hero and his legend grew. Peasants claimed he turned into an agave plant when U.S. troops were near. Or he turned into a barking dog and nipped at the heels of the soldiers' horses as they passed through town.

From a military standpoint, the Pershing Expedition wasn't a success. They put the elusive Villa to flight but never captured him. In February 1916, President Wilson recalled the Expedition. Bigger things were brewing in Europe.

In Arizona, rumors spread that Villa was planning to enter the state with a large army, blow up Roosevelt Dam, and rob banks in Phoenix and Tucson. The National Guard was mobilized and some four hundred men trained for the raid that never came.

Over There

GERMANY WAS DOING EVERYTHING in her power to encourage the Mexicans to do battle along the Mexican border, thus keeping American troops from going "Over There." They were so encouraged by the seemingly inept U.S. Army being unable to capture a Mexican bandit that they resumed unrestricted submarine warfare on American shipping.

The Germans miscalculated. Pershing's Punitive Expedition proved to be a good training ground for American soldiers, and it gave birth to the aviation section of the Signal Corps, the future Air Force. It was an

An "American Sunday" parade was held in Tucson on April 1, 1917, just five days before America entered the "war to end all wars". Tucson's population was 23,000 at the time, yet more than 15,000 American flags were sold.

unceremonious beginning, as the entire First Aero Squadron consisting of eight Curtis JN2s was completely destroyed. They weren't shot down by enemy fire, however; most were blown out of the sky by the wild winds of Chihuahua, while others were damaged during landings on the rough terrain.

Arizonans and their fellow Southwesterners were not especially keen on going to war in Europe. Eastern businesses were making huge profits selling goods to both sides, so the general feeling out West was, "let the Easterners fight the war." Or that was the feeling until British Naval Intelligence intercepted a note from the German Minister of Foreign Affairs, Arthur Zimmermann, to the German minister in Mexico City, instructing him to propose an alliance with Venustiano Carranza. If Mexico would stir up trouble along the border, Texas, Arizona, and New Mexico would be returned to them following a German victory in Europe. The note gave Arizonans a patriotic jolt and raised the fighting blood of all Southwesterners. They began to volunteer in droves.

"RECONQUERED ARIZONA TO BE PART OF MEXICO'S REWARD" screamed the headlines of the *Arizona Republican* (which would later become the *Republic*) on the morning of March 1, 1917. Up to that time the German ambassador to the United States, Count Johann von Bernstorff, had been assuring the Americans that Germany wanted peace with this nation. Wilson had wanted to avoid war with Germany if possible, but after the release of the Zimmermann note a declaration of war was inevitable.

The Battle of Ambos Nogales

WHEN THE UNITED STATES DECLARED WAR on Germany on April 6, 1917, veterans of the Punitive Expedition to Mexico had just settled in at Fort Huachuca. They were anxious to head for France and get a crack at Kaiser Bill. Most of the black troopers of the famous Tenth Cavalry never got the chance, as things were still hot along the border. During the summer of 1918, intelligence reports noted the presence of well-armed Mexicans in the vicinity of Nogales. Among them were a number of Germans. This was not surprising since German agents had been active in all the border towns during the past four years. An anonymous letter from a disgruntled ex-*Villista* warned of an outbreak against the U.S. at Nogales sometime in August.

On the afternoon of August 27, a Mexican national crossed over the border, ignoring the warnings of customs guards to halt. When a guard and a soldier went in pursuit, a Mexican customs guard opened fire, killing the soldier. As other Mexicans rushed up to join the melee, American soldiers returned fire, killing several. The Battle of Ambos Nogales had commenced.

Troops at nearby Camp Little were alerted. Three troops of the Tenth Cavalry rode at a gallop into Nogales, followed by three companies of infantry. U.S. soldiers were posted strategically on the high slopes facing the Mexican border. Civilians trying to assist got into the act, running wildly in the streets and firing pistols and rifles erratically across the border. The well-meaning but trigger-happy civilians were rounded up and confined to the city hall.

Heavy gunfire commenced from the Mexican side. Bullets pounded the walls of houses and buildings. From the roof of the Concordia Hotel snipers opened fire.

By 6:00 P.M. a large force of Americans occupied several strategic points on the Mexican side. Mexican losses were high, and the commander ran up a white flag but failed to call on his soldiers to cease fire. A conference was held, and the Mexican officer audaciously ordered the Americans to throw down their guns and surrender. Furthermore, he threatened to disarm them himself. The sudden presence of Tenth Cavalry troops discouraged him from pursuing the matter.

That night a trainload of Mexican reinforcements arrived from Hermosillo. They were greeted by a machine-gun company and several more troops of cavalry just arrived from Fort Huachuca. Deciding that discretion was the better part of valor, they retreated. The Battle of Ambos Nogales ended.

Mexican casualties were high. Their losses were nearly a hundred, including the town mayor. German agents had played a prominent role in engineering the battle. Among the dead Mexicans were two German agents provocateurs. American losses were two officers and three enlisted men killed, along with several civilians, and twenty-nine men wounded.

A Busy Year

THE YEAR 1917 was an eventful one for Arizonans. America declared war on Germany; more than a thousand miners were deported by rail from Bisbee; public drinking cups and community bar towels were banned. The Copper Queen Consolidated Copper Company began calling itself the Phelps Dodge Corporation, and many predicted the name wouldn't stick. That year the legislature passed a ten-dollar-a-week minimum wage for women and adopted a state flag. (The flag inspired some protesting, as many felt it looked too much like the Japanese flag.) Authorities in the border town of Nogales complained their jails were overflowing with draft dodgers from all over the country. The sheriff of Pinal County saw fit to pour twenty thousand dollars' worth of booze on the courthouse lawn. The state of Arizona was only five years old and wasn't off to a very good start.

It was also the year for one of the most bizarre incidents in Arizona politics. In the 1916 gubernatorial election Republican Tom Campbell and Democrat George W. P. Hunt finished in a virtual tie. The courts then determined that Campbell had won by some thirty votes. But Hunt, the incumbent, refused to vacate his office.

Both men took the oath of office in separate ceremonies on January 1, and both men got up to address the opening session of the legislature. Campbell ran the state out of his home, while Hunt remained in the capitol building. The state treasurer, a Democrat, refused to honor checks signed by Campbell. Hunt demanded a recount but again came up thirty votes short. He then went to court, but the judge ruled Campbell the winner. Still Hunt wouldn't surrender his office, appealing to the State Supreme Court, which ruled in December in favor of Hunt on the grounds that many Democrats marked their ballots for "straight ticket," then proceeded to vote for Campbell, the Republican. The court threw those ballots out, and Hunt had enough votes to keep the office. For eleven months, the state had two governors and things were still a mess.

THE STATE FLAG

✳ Arizona's flag was approved by the state legislature on March 9, 1915, and became official in 1917. The flag's lower half is a blue field. The top half represents the rays of an Arizona sunset, and the copper star symbolizes what was historically the state's most important industry. The colors red and gold represent the colors carried by the first Spanish explorers in 1540, under the command of Francisco Vasquez de Coronado in his quest for the fabled seven cities of Cibola. Blue and gold are the state colors. The thirteen red and gold rays equal the number of stripes on the U.S. flag. The red and blue are designated the same colors as on the U.S. flag.

The flag was designed in 1910 by Colonel Charles Wilfred Harris for the Arizona National Guard rifle team. Members of the team suggested the emblem after attending the national rifle matches at Camp Perry, Ohio, where the team from Arizona was the only one without a flag. The flag was sewn by Nancy Hayden, the wife of team member and Senator-to-be Carl Hayden. Thus she became the state's own Betsy Ross.

When the flag was first adopted there was much criticism from those who thought it too closely resembled the Japanese flag. In the South Pacific during WWII, the flag wasn't displayed in combat zones for fear of its being fired upon mistakenly.

Arizona's Service in the Great War

FOLLOWING THE DECLARATION OF WAR, Arizonans, along with their fellow Americans, rallied around the flag. More Arizonans per capita, some twelve thousand, served in the armed forces than any other state. The 158th Arizona National Guard was mobilized and sent to Europe as part of the 40th Division. After the war the 158th was selected as President Wilson's special honor guard in Paris.

Thousands of American women said good-bye to their men as they boarded troopships heading for Europe. At least one, a twenty-two-year old housewife from Douglas, chose to "stand by her man." On July 24, 1917, she was sent home after stowing away with her husband on a troopship.

The impact of three long years of warfare had taken its toll on the English and French armies. The arrival of the American Expeditionary Force under the leadership of General John J. Pershing was a welcome sight.

The first Arizonan of the 321 to fall in battle was a Pima Indian, Matthew Juan of Sacaton. He was also the first American Indian to die in the war.

John Henry Pruitt, USMC, of Camp Verde won the Congressional Medal of Honor posthumously.

Lt. Frank Luke, Jr., scion of a pioneer Phoenix family, was one of America's greatest heroes of the war. Luke was a natural leader, a star football player for

Matthew Juan.

Phoenix Union High School. After graduation in 1915 he took a job working in the mines at Ajo.

He enlisted as a private in the Signal Corps in September 25, 1917, and was able to get a commission and join the aviation section as a pilot. Fighter planes were fragile little ships in those days and were known to fall apart in midair. It took a lot of courage just to go up in one of them.

Luke was fiercely independent and was branded a maverick by his superior officers. On his first combat mission he left formation, claiming engine trouble, and went out on his own. Then he did it again. When his commanding officer confronted him, Luke's response was, "I got a Hun." Soon, the daring pilot was going after the German observation balloons, earning himself the nickname, the "Balloon Buster From Arizona." Observation balloons were the terror of infantry men. From their aerial advantage they could direct artillery fire down on the trenches. They were also well-protected by antiaircraft guns and fighter planes. Luke was becoming a legend on the western front.

When Luke's flying partner and fellow ace, Lt. Joe Wehner, was shot down Luke became even more obsessed with downing German aircraft. He'd also become depressed over the loss of his friend. Luke's commanding officer sent his young ace on leave, but he soon returned from Paris saying, "There was nothing to do."

Luke went back in action with a new partner, but he too was shot down. Now Luke became a lone hunter with a vengeance, making unauthorized flights and shooting down enemy aircraft. On September 29,

Frank Luke, WWI Fighter Ace.

COWBOY BALLADEERS

✳ *Another Arizona soldier, Gail Gardner of Prescott, was a Dartmouth-educated cowboy with a degree in math. After college he returned to Prescott and started a cattle ranch. In those days, Prescott's Whiskey Row had forty saloons, and cowboys in town on a spree took up the challenge of trying to have at least one drink in each saloon. Gardner claimed he and his partner, Sandy Bob Heckle, had done that one Saturday night, and on the way back to their ranch the next morning the devil jumped out of a hole in the ground and tried to haul the sinful cowboys off to hell. Undaunted, the fearless cowboys grabbed their ropes. One roped the devil's horns while the other roped his hind feet. They treated old Lucifer like a wild cow, tipping his horns, ear-marking him, and branding him. Then, for a final insult, they tied knots in his tail.*

When war came, Gardner joined the Army Signal Corps. While riding a troop train across Kansas he got lonesome for the cattle ranges of Yavapai County, so he sat down and wrote the words to a poem, "Sierry Petes" or "Tyin' Knots in the Devil's Tail." Sierry Petes is cowboy lingo for the Sierra Prieta Mountains near Prescott. In the poem, Buster Jig is Gardner and Sandy Bob is Bob Heckle. (Heckle was an uncle to country music legend Marty Robbins.)

Gardner's poem was set to music by another cowboy, Billy Simon, and later recorded by a number of cowboy singers, including Rex Allen. It remains one of America's most popular cowboy songs.

Luke was grounded, but despite the order he went to his Spad XIII and took off on another unauthorized flight. He dropped a message to the ground observers: "Watch three Hun balloons on the Meuse. Luke." And off he went.

Luke flamed all three balloons and shot down two enemy planes, but his own ship was hit by ground fire and he was wounded. Luke was running short of fuel but before landing, he spotted some German infantry, so he swooped down and strafed them.

When Luke landed in a church cemetery vengeful enemy troops quickly surrounded his downed plane. Luke knew he had little chance to surrender since he'd just killed several of their comrades in the strafing, so he drew his pistol and elected to shoot it out. After a brief firefight, he was killed.

On that fateful day, in just ten minutes of action, Frank Luke, Jr. had gunned down two planes and three balloons.

The French residents of a nearby village later said his body was stripped of all decorations and identification, placed in a wheelbarrow, and paraded through the village. Afterward the Germans left the body to be buried by the villagers. Luke's body was not located until May 1919, several months after the war ended.

In battle there is sometimes a very thin line between a hero and a court-martial. It's likely that if Luke had returned from his last flight he would have been arrested and court-martialed. Instead, he became the first aviator to be awarded the Congressional Medal of Honor. Luke Air Force Base was named in his honor, and his statue graces the entrance to the capitol building in Phoenix.

Lt. Frank Luke, Jr. and Captain Eddie Rickenbacker, who downed twenty-six enemy planes, were the only two American aviators to win the Congressional Medal of Honor in the First World War.

On the Home Front

THE MOST TRAUMATIC EVENT in Arizona's labor history was the infamous Bisbee Deportation in 1917. For years a bitter struggle was waged

Deportation of strike sympathizers, July 12, 1917.

between the unions and mining companies. It came to a head during World War I at Bisbee. The price of copper was skyrocketing and profits were up, but the mine workers felt their lot was no better. The companies insisted the men ought to be doing their part for the war effort and that any talk of strike was unpatriotic.

Phelps Dodge, the company that owned most of the mines around Bisbee, decided to take action. On July 12, 1917, at 6:30 A.M., two thousand armed men, white handkerchiefs tied around their upper arms for identification, took to the streets of Bisbee and rounded up some two thousand suspected strike sympathizers. They were herded to the baseball park at Warren, and by day's end some twelve hundred were loaded up on railroad cars and shipped east to Columbus, New Mexico. It was a miracle that only two men, one vigilante and one alleged striker, died in the affair.

In the end Phelps Dodge was victorious and the unions were broken. It was a severe setback for the unions, and it would be many years before they would regain any real bargaining power.

The Last Lynching

IN 1916 ARIZONANS rescinded capital punishment in a close vote. Ironically, that might have led to the state's last lynching. On the evening of May 3, 1917, a mysterious itinerant named Starr Daley came upon a young couple from Tucson camped along the old Apache Trail. Daley shot James Roy Gibson in the back four times. Then he raped and abducted his wife, Florence. He donned the slain man's clothes and told Mrs. Gibson they were going to Oklahoma, posing as husband and wife. She refused to do anything until the body of her husband was taken to a mortuary in Mesa, the nearest town. This Daley unwittingly agreed to do. As a criminal, he wasn't the sharpest knife in the drawer.

Before they could begin, Mrs. Gibson had to teach Daley to drive the car. In downtown Mesa, the car ran out of gas. Daley left her alone in the car while he went for gas. This gave Mrs. Gibson a chance to alert a passerby to her plight. Lawmen arrived soon after, and Daley was arrested without incident. He was taken to the Phoenix city jail, where a lynch mob of some five hundred angry men soon gathered. The mob demanded an eye for an eye, though the death penalty in Arizona had been rescinded just a year earlier.

Maricopa County Sheriff W. H. Wilky sent out a decoy car and then tried to sneak Daley out the back way to take him to the state prison in Florence, but the ruse didn't work. A caravan of angry vigilantes chased the lawmen and Daley through the streets of Tempe and Mesa in what must have looked like something out of a cops-and-robbers movie. In the early morning hours of May 6, 1917, the small motorcade was halted outside Florence, and Daley was taken by the vigilantes to the site of the murder near Superstition Mountain.

Most unusual about this lynching was that Daley had to show his executioners how to fashion a hangman's noose so that it would snap his neck rather than strangle him. He then suggested they use a car and the cross arm of a telephone pole as a makeshift gallows.

The cause of death was determined to be at the hands of unknown individuals, and no attempt was ever made to prosecute the vigilantes.

The Power Brothers

ONE OF THE STATE'S most sensational and controversial gunfights occurred in 1918. Tom and John Power lived with their father, Jeff, and an old army scout named Tom Sisson in a mining cabin high up in the remote Galiuro Mountains. When the two boys didn't report for the draft, a posse went up from Safford to arrest them. The posse, U.S. Marshal Frank Haynes, Graham County Sheriff Frank McBride, Chief Deputy Martin Kempton, and Kane Wooten, rode into Rattlesnake Canyon on the snowy morning of February 10, 1918. They left their horses picketed in the brush nearby and approached the cabin on foot. As they attempted to surround the dwelling, a bell mare spooked and the noise alerted the men inside. Jeff Power stepped into the doorway to see what spooked the mare and shots rang out. He fell, mortally wounded.

Inside the cabin Tom and John sprang from their beds, grabbed their rifles, and jacked shells into the chambers. Bullets slammed into the cabin, shattering windows and splintering wood. Outside a heavy fog blanketed the area. A shadowy figure moved, and Tom drew a bead, then squeezed the trigger. The figure dropped in the snow and didn't move. Several more shots rang out, and then a deathly silence prevailed. When the smoke cleared, all the posse was dead except Marshal Frank Haynes. He lit out for the town of Klondyke without actually seeing the gunfight (it was very foggy and Haynes had approached the cabin from a different direction than the rest) and reported the Powers had ambushed his posse.

The news spread like wildfire, and in the spirit of patriotism, the largest manhunt in Arizona thus began for the alleged draft dodgers. For the next twenty-nine days posse groups scoured the mountains and deserts of the Southwest in search of the Power brothers and Tom Sisson. The trio was finally captured a few miles below the Mexican border.

MARY JANE ELIZABETH COLTER

✳ *Millions of people who visit the Grand Canyon each year pass through buildings designed by Mary Jane Elizabeth Colter. Colter's buildings blend harmoniously with their beautiful surroundings. According to her biographer, Virginia Grattan, "Colter's philosophy was that a building should grow out of its setting, embodying the history and flavor of the location. . . . It should belong to its environment as though indigenous to that spot."*

Colters' career in Southwest architecture began in 1902, when she took a summer job working for Fred Harvey. Two years later she was commissioned to build the Hopi House at Grand Canyon, a building that she patterned after the ancient Hopi structures at Oraibi on Third Mesa.

In 1910 the Fred Harvey Company hired her full time, and she worked for the company for the next forty-six years. During those years, she was responsible for twenty-one projects, including seven more buildings at the Grand Canyon (Lookout Studio, Hermit's Rest, Phantom Ranch, Desert View Watchtower, Bright Angel Lodge, and two employee dormitories), La Posada in Winslow, and the Painted Desert Inn at Petrified Forest National Park.

She died in Santa Fe on January 8, 1956, but her legacy continues. Many other national parks use designs based on the native stone and rough-hewn style of architecture, following the philosophy of Colter.

The trial caused a sensation. Because of the prominence of the slain lawmen and the fact that the boys were accused of dodging the draft, the trial was an open-and-shut case. The boys would have been hanged had the death penalty not been rescinded. Instead they were given life sentences.

In another time the Power brothers and Tom Sisson might have been found not guilty. They claimed no knowledge of having to report for the draft and had only returned fire in self-defense, having no idea who was shooting at them.

The Power brothers spent thirty-four years behind bars before being given a clemency hearing and would serve a total of forty-two years before they would be released. The average time for a "lifer" was only seven years. The brothers were given full pardons in 1969. Both died soon after. Sisson died in prison in 1957.

But in 1918, angry that the boys were only given life sentences and still smarting over the Starr Daley murder, Arizonans reinstated the death penalty.

Grand Canyon National Park

IN 1869 JOHN WESLEY POWELL and his band of adventurers went down the Colorado River in boats, becoming (arguably) the first explorers in the Grand Canyon. It was Powell who named it and who vividly depicted its awe-inspiring beauty in his reports, awakening the interest of many, including President Theodore Roosevelt, who made it a National Monument in 1908.

For a time the Canyon's resources were exploited as miners dug for minerals and others proposed building a railroad through it. But thanks to the Santa Fe Railroad, the Fred Harvey Company, and others, tourists were already traveling to the Canyon, and National Park status was granted in 1919 to save it from irreparable damage due to commercial exploitation. In that year, less than 45,000 people visited. Today more than twice that number visit each day.

AS THE DECADE WOUND DOWN, Arizonans, like their fellow Americans, turned their attention away from troubles abroad and looked to the future. They felt secure in the knowledge that they had done their share in the "Great War to End All Wars," the war that would make the world safe for democracy.

THE DECADE THAT ROARED

"The business of America is business."

—President Calvin Coolidge in a January 17, 1925 speech

"Wall Street Lays an Egg"

—Variety, commenting on the 1929 stock market crash

E ACH NEW DECADE BEGINS with a census, and the census of 1920 presented a changing of the guard in Arizona. The "Mother of Cities," the Old Pueblo of Tucson, would relinquish its title as largest city in Arizona to that upstart to the north, Phoenix. Tucson didn't give up the title quietly. A newspaper article published on May 12, 1920, said: "Tucson accuses Phoenix of holding up the release of its population numbers until after Tucson so it can show a larger number." When the final tally was recorded, Phoenix counted 29,000 residents while Tucson had only 20,292.

Today there are those who swear it's impossible to purchase a compass in Tucson because merchants refuse to sell anything that points to Phoenix. A story is told that a reporter once asked the mayor of Tucson to comment on the number of people moving from his community to Phoenix, and his comment was: "It raises the IQ in both places."

After the War

THE SHORTAGES CREATED during the First World War had put the country in a self-denying mood. War needs had caused the government to prohibit the use of grain for making liquor. The culmination of century-old reform movements helped add two new amendments to the Constitution. In January 1919, two-thirds of the states ratified the Eighteenth Amendment, which prohibited the "manufacture, sale, and transportation" of alcoholic beverages.

War conditions also advanced the cause of women's rights. Women had taken over jobs in factories usually held by men and had served valiantly behind the lines in the war. Women would no longer be denied the right to vote, and in 1920, the Nineteenth Amendment was passed, granting suffrage.

President Wilson, his health broken, was unable to govern the country the last year and a half of his term. His single-minded goal was getting the United States into the League of Nations. He was convinced the nation should not retreat from world leadership. On the other hand, most Americans wanted a return to the good old days.

Frederick Allen said it best in *Only Yesterday:* "The nation was spiritually tired. Wearied by the excitements of the war and the nervous tension of the Big Red Scare, they hoped for quiet and healing. Sick of Wilson and his talk of America's duty to humanity, they hoped for a chance to pursue their private affairs without government interference and to forget about public affairs. There might be no such word in the dictionary as normalcy, but normalcy was what they wanted."

As America greeted the 1920s it hung suspended between adolescence and maturity. Skepticism prevailed. Most Americans believed the world's problems were too complex to settle and favored

"Hip Hop" of the 1920s.

isolationism. The Bolshevik Revolution that overthrew the czar in Russia caused a so-called Red Scare in this country. There was a brief panic when, in 1920, an anarchist exploded a bomb on Wall Street, killing thirty people. Following a brief, postwar depression, the economy bounced back. The Communist scare vanished and materialism flourished.

Young Americans were ready to let their hair down and cast off the customs and mores of the past. In the spirit of frivolity, girls began bobbing their hair at ear level, rolling down their stockings, and hemming their dresses at the knees. Outrageous fashion was the rage. Men wore "oxford bags," pants characterized by big, oversized legs, not unlike today's "hip-hop" trousers. Cigarette smoking became more popular than ever as more women took up the habit. Cigarette sales doubled during the decade.

Arizona Goes Dry

WITH THE PASSING of the Eighteenth Amendment in 1920, drinking alcoholic beverages became a federal offense. Clandestine drinking had great appeal to the hedonists of the twenties. The older generation scorned the young men and women who drank bathtub gin, carried hip flasks, visited speakeasies, and danced scandalous dances like the fox-trot and the Charleston. Mothers, fearing the worst, wouldn't let their daughters leave the house without man-discouraging underwear. But as soon as these flapper girls got to the dance, the first thing they did was head for the ladies' room and "park their girdles."

Five years before the passing of Prohibition Arizona went "dry," on January 1, 1915.

Supporters for Prohibition take their cause to the streets of
Phoenix to celebrate the state going dry in 1915.

Bars closed their doors and the bootlegging industry began. Moonshine stills flourished everywhere, from remote desert washes to the rugged mountains of the state. In Scottsdale, moonshiners buried their stills in nearby Indian Bend Wash. Here, agents or "prohibs" used rebar to probe the sand for stills. Pleasant Valley had such a reputation for whiskey stills that it was proposed at a public meeting in Globe that a pipeline be built from Young to satisfy the needs of the thirsty imbibers in the county seat. In Phoenix, liquor agents seized some illegal booze in a local hotel and were pouring it down an upstairs bathtub when they discovered some enterprising em-ployees had tapped into the drainpipes and were diverting the hooch into another reservoir.

Flapper girl flashing secret flask.

Flickers and Talkies

SINCE THE BARS WERE CLOSED, people sought entertainment elsewhere, and Hollywood stepped up to fill the gap. The earliest movies, called flickers, were shown mostly in makeshift buildings. The price of admission was five cents, hence the name "nickelodeons." In 1913 the Elks Theater in Phoenix thrilled audiences with a kinetophone, invented by Thomas Edison. It consisted of a film projector and a phonograph running in unison. By the time the war ended regular theaters were showing full-length movies.

The silent film era ended in 1927 with *The Jazz Singer,* starring Al Jolson. Motion pictures had become big business, the nation's fourth largest industry, and elaborate movie palaces were being built all over the country. By 1929 Phoenix had seven theaters, including the beautiful

Mae West or a look-alike at the Orpheum Theater, 1929.

Orpheum, with its Mayan idols, electric fountains, and ceiling with blinking stars and rolling clouds. Five thousand people were turned away on opening night. By the end of the decade some ninety million people nationwide were heading to theaters each week to view the talkies.

The newfangled motion pictures created a whole new form of entertainment for cowboys, too. In the early days, a cowboy coming into town had little else to do but get cleaned up, hit the saloons, then visit the ladies on the line. Now they could see a movie, too. A story is told of a cowboy going into a Flagstaff theater to see his first movie. He sat in the front row and watched wide-eyed as an array of beautiful young women strolled down to a country swimming hole where they began to disrobe. Just as they got to the interesting part, a freight train rolled by, blocking the view. After the movie, the cowboy went to the ticket office and asked to purchase six more tickets.

"Why would you want to do that," the cashier asked, "when we're showing the same movie over and over?"

"I don't know anything about these newfangled motion pictures," the cowboy assured her, "but I do know something about trains. Sooner or later one of 'em's gonna be late, and I aim to be there when it happens."

Hard-Riding Heroes of the Silver Screen

HOLLYWOOD's hard-riding heroes of the silver screen, Tom Mix, Hoot Gibson, Buck Jones, and Ken Maynard, made movies around Prescott and nearby Granite Dells. Of these four, the most famous was Tom Mix. His life story, as it was told, was partly truth and partly fiction. His agent claimed, among other things, that he'd been a Texas Ranger, rode with Pancho Villa, and fought in the Boer and Spanish-American wars. All this was fiction, but one thing was certain: Mix could ride a horse with the best of them. To be a shooting star in those days of silent films was more important than acting. His co-star was Tony, the most famous horse in the movies.

Tom Mix and Tony.

Mix got his start as a trick rider in the Miller Brothers Wild West show. By the early 1920s, he was earning $17,000 a week cranking out two-reelers. Many of Tom Mix's three hundred movies were filmed around Prescott, and he was no stranger to the town. In 1909 he won the national rodeo championship at Prescott's Frontier Days Rodeo. During breaks he'd entertain the Prescottonians with his prowess atop Tony. Mix would toss his hat on the ground and then, riding at a full gallop, reach down from the saddle and scoop it up.

The late-great Prescott historian Lester "Budge" Ruffner told a story of how all the children would try to imitate Mix's feats. The end result was broken arms or worse. Ruffner claimed angry mothers blamed Mix and threatened to throw an old-fashioned lynching party for the famous movie star.

Mix's fabulous movie career ended with the era of silent films. The rough-and-tumble cowboy had a high-pitched voice and, as with many other stars of the time, it didn't work in the talkies. After his movie days were over, Mix spent a lot of time in the state as an entertainer. He was killed near Florence in 1940, when his Ford convertible flipped on the highway south of town.

The Bambino Comes to Phoenix

IN SPORTS, THE 1920S was the heroic era, the age of legends. And the quintessence of them all was the immortal George Herman "Babe" Ruth. The Babe best symbolized the great love affair between the American public and sports stars of the twenties. He hit sixty home runs in 1927, a record that held for more than thirty years. His career mark of 714 home runs lasted even longer. Perhaps most important, he almost single-handedly restored the grand image of the national pastime from the depths of the notorious Black Sox Scandal of the 1919 World Series.

The Bambino came into the big leagues with the Boston Red Sox in 1914 as a pitcher. He might have been one of the all-time great hurlers (his record for pitching twenty-five scoreless innings while leading the Red Sox to World Championships in 1916 and 1918 stood for more than thirty years), but his skill with a bat made him an everyday player. The Red Sox traded him to the New York Yankees in 1920 for $100,000, twice the amount ever paid for a ball player. That year, he hit fifty-four home runs for the Bronx Bombers, more than any other team in the American League. In 1927, the Babe hit sixty home runs, setting a record that lasted until Roger Maris hit sixty-one in 1961.

Ruth's flamboyant lifestyle both on and off the field was the stuff of legends and set the standard for

Babe Ruth, perhaps the greatest superstar of them all, entertained Arizonans in 1926 with his hitting skills.

the Roaring Twenties. Arizonans got a firsthand look at the mighty Babe in 1926, when he and a beautiful woman companion were on their way by passenger train to Mexico. When the train pulled into Phoenix the Yankee slugger noticed some youngsters playing baseball in a nearby field. He stepped down off the train, picked up a bat, and commenced launching baseballs into a cotton field some four hundred feet away.

AIN'T WE GOT FUN

☀ Much of the upheaval that was shaking up America's morals was occurring on college campuses. The times gave rise to Greek fraternities and sororities. A few years earlier, in 1912, the University of Arizona banned ragtime music on the campus. College kids of the twenties owned cars, sported raccoon coats, and had money to spend. They prided themselves as cynics and professed to be uninterested in politics. The chorus of a popular song of the day, "In the meantime, in-between time, ain't we got fun," seem to fit the mood. Other "barbaric" tunes that reflected the period were: "Runnin' Wild," "Yes Sir, That's My Baby," "Ukulele Lady," "Gimme a Little Kiss, Will Ya, Huh?" and "Sweet Georgia Brown."

Cotton and Copper

THE WAR HAD CREATED a huge market in Arizona for cotton, cattle, lumber, and copper. Prices were at an all-time high. Cotton, needed as fabric for airplanes and military uniforms, replaced alfalfa as the major agricultural crop, selling at a dollar a pound. Farmers moved to Arizona from Texas, took out mortgages in communities like Scottsdale, planted crops, and paid off their mortgages when those crops came in. A new type of cotton, Pima long staple, was developed.

Cotton was also in demand as cord in the new inflatable automobile tires and Arizona's first cotton king wasn't a farmer. Paul Litchfield was with the Goodyear Tire and Rubber Company. In 1916 he bought 24,000 acres of land in Chandler and the west end of the Salt River Valley, where Litchfield Park is today. He cleared the land, dug wells and irrigation ditches, and planted long staple cotton.

The boom didn't last long. Egyptian cotton became available after the war, and new spinning methods reduced the need for long staple cotton. Hard times fell on cotton farmers as markets collapsed. They began to diversify, planting more citrus and vegetable crops as health-conscious Americans began to change their eating habits. Still, cotton would remain Arizona's major agricultural crop.

By the end of the war most of the rich underground copper mines in Arizona were almost played out. The advent of trucks and steam shovels, along with other earth-moving equipment, changed mining dramatically. Open-pit mining made low-grade ore profitable. A Bisbee landmark known as Sacramento Hill eventually became the Sacramento Pit.

In 1929 there were less than three hundred miles of paved highway in Arizona.
Horses were still the most reliable means of transportation.

The wartime demand for copper had driven the price up to twenty-seven cents a pound; however, during the postwar depression the price dropped to less than half that amount, causing the mines to close operations temporarily.

The copper industry got a boost during the 1920s when Americans went on a buying spree. The installment plan was introduced and soon became the rage. Products such as automobiles, toasters, radios, refrigerators, and washing machines all used copper in their manufacturing.

The livestock and lumber industry also shared in the prosperity of the war and the bust that followed. Lumbering, which had begun in Flagstaff in the 1880s, spread to the White Mountains.

The Golden Age of Automobiles

IN 1924 EVERY OTHER CAR in the world was a Ford Model T. By 1929 a finished car was rolling off the Ford assembly line every seventeen seconds. By then the automobile was America's biggest industry, with twenty-six million cars and trucks registered. The automobile also opened the door for other kinds of businesses: garages, motor courts (motels), road house cafés, and gas stations.

The automobile changed life in Arizona during the twenties. In 1920 there were only 34,619 cars registered in the state. By the end of the decade the number had risen to over 120,000, including trucks and other commercial vehicles like buses and taxis. With more autos came the demand for more and

Fixing a flat on a trip through southern Arizona, 1926.

better roads. Gasoline taxes were levied after 1921 for highway construction. In 1925 the national highway system began and primary roads became part of the U.S. Highway system.

In northern Arizona, the old Beale wagon road and proposed railroad route, which had been surveyed during the 1850s by the Army Corps of Topographical Engineers, became the fabled Route 66 in 1926. Federal monies provided during the Depression caused the road to be completely paved by 1938. Army engineers had also surveyed a southern route along the thirty-second parallel in southern Arizona. It became U.S. Highway 80. (Today these are Interstates 40, 10, and 8.)

In 1929 the Navajo Bridge crossing Marble Canyon was completed, opening up the Arizona Strip and the North Rim of the Grand Canyon for tourism. Prior to that, travelers between the Arizona Strip and the rest of Arizona had to cross the Colorado River on a ferry at historic Lee's Ferry, the route used by Mormon colonists following the Hamblin Trail into Arizona from Utah beginning in the 1870s. The route was familiarly known as the Honeymoon Trail for all the young Mormon couples who traveled back up the trail from Arizona to have their marriage vows sanctified in the temple at St. George, Utah. The Honeymoon Trail experience ended with the completion of the Mormon Temple at Mesa in 1926.

The spectacular canyon now spanned by Navajo Bridge marks the north entrance to the Grand Canyon, and was named by John Wesley Powell. The one-armed explorer looked up at the titanic cliffs and believed them to be marble. In 1925 the United States Geological Survey officially named the canyon Marble Gorge. (The name was changed to Marble Canyon in 1961, and eight years later it became a national monument.)

In Maricopa County more than three hundred miles of concrete roads, only sixteen feet wide, were built in the early 1920s to aid farmers getting their goods to market. By the end of the decade, the state had more than two thousand miles of roads. Most, however, were gravel surfaced. Less than three hundred miles of paved highways existed in the state; 138 miles were paved with concrete and another 162 had asphalt paving.

Aviation Adventures and Misadventures

THE DECADE was the age of aviation. The "Lone Eagle," Charles Lindbergh, became the first to fly solo across the Atlantic. In planes held together with ingenuity and baling wire, barnstormers flew around the country putting on aerobatics shows. Because of the clear skies and wide open spaces, Arizona was a favorite place for aviators to ply their trade. Barnstorming pilots put on aerial shows throughout the state. Flying war surplus Curtiss JN-4D trainers purchased for three hundred dollars, they'd first do a flyover, then buzz the town. A stunt man would walk on a wing or parachute to the ground. Then the plane would land, and folks would line up to go up in the air, paying five dollars for five minutes in the sky.

Bill Gilpin of Bisbee was a pilot who hired out as chauffeur for copper magnate John Greenway. He soon convinced the ex–Rough Rider that it would be much faster traveling from one mining operation to another in a plane instead of an automobile. When Greenway died in 1926, Gilpin persuaded his widow, Isabella, to partner up with him in a charter airline. They called it G & G Airlines, but it was better known as Gilpin Airlines and soon became one of the biggest fixed-base operations in the Southwest.

Gilpin Airfield was located northwest of the Tucson city limits. (During the 1940s a youngster attending Tucson High School, future astronaut Frank Borman would take his first flying lessons at the airfield.) Gilpin Airlines did well flying Americans into prohibition-free Mexico. Gilpin was killed while making a landing in Mexico during a storm, and Mrs. Greenway sold the operation. (During the 1930s she would represent the state in Congress.)

The pride of Italy, the *Santa Maria,* became the first seaplane to fly into Arizona on February 13, 1927. Throngs of people, including many Italians, made the long, dusty six-hour trip up the Apache Trail to Roosevelt Lake to see the plane. The ship landed smoothly on the lake and was refueling when it caught fire and burned before horrified spectators. The whole event took about ten minutes, and no one was injured, including the pilot. There was talk that the plane was sabotaged by those who hated Fascist leader Benito Mussolini. An international incident was averted by a reporter for *The Arizona Republican* (later the *Republic*). He discovered that a worker had accidentally tossed his cigarette into the gas-covered waters of the lake. The plane's pilot, a pal of Il Duce, had poured the gas onto the lake himself.

The *Santa Maria* had been a leading contender to be the first to fly the Atlantic, but the fire twisted the tale of fate, and the first to fly it was Lindbergh. It's likely that the Italian pilot, General Francesco de Pinedo, was no longer a member in good standing in Mussolini's inner group.

One of the most bizarre incidents in Arizona's aeronautical history occurred on September 16, 1927, when stunt pilot Marty Jensen was chosen by MGM to fly their famous lion, Leo, cross-country on a promotional junket. (Three years earlier Jensen and his wife, Peg, were married in a Jenny while flying over Yuma. The cockpit was so small that Marty had to sit on his bride's lap while the judge performed the ceremony sitting in the backseat. Because there was no room for a witness on the plane, a second ceremony was held on the ground.)

The flight from Los Angeles to New York with Leo was a wobbly one. The lion weighed about four hundred pounds and the protective glass cage weighed another four hundred. When they hit the hot desert air the plane began to lose altitude. It struggled past Phoenix and flew low through a pass in the Mazatzals. With the forbidding Mogollon Rim ahead, Jensen was boxed in. He stalled and crashed into the top of a huge oak tree a few miles from Kohl's Ranch, then crawled out of the wreckage. Fortunately, the cage remained intact and Leo was shaken but okay.

Jensen started walking through the wilderness, hoping to find help. Two days later he was still walking. Finally, he came upon a ranch, and messages were relayed to MGM and to his wife, who'd already set out in another plane to find him. She was in Phoenix when word arrived that he was alive.

The rescue party reached Leo and found the famous lion weak but alive. He spent the next few days being pampered and fed by the good people of Payson. Leo, the ferocious MGM lion, turned out to be a good-natured pussycat who enjoyed milk and sandwiches. Everybody in Payson, particularly the children, were sorry to see him return to Hollywood. The wreckage of Jensen's plane can still be seen in Hell's Canyon near Payson.

By 1928 an airline called Scenic Airways was carrying five thousand

LUCKY LINDY

✳ *Charles Lindbergh, recently returned from his historic solo flight across the Atlantic, dedicated Arizona's new Davis-Monthan airfield in 1927. More than twelve thousand fans showed up to meet the famous aviator as he landed in his silver-tinted monoplane, the* Spirit of St. Louis. *At that time Davis-Monthan was the nation's largest airfield. A year later Lindbergh selected northern Arizona as a route for a new coast-to-coast airline, Transcontinental Air Transport Company. When the first flight was made in 1929, "America's Sweetheart" Mary Pickford christened the plane piloted by Lucky Lindy. He was accompanied by another famous pilot, Amelia Earhart. That same year, Lindbergh and his wife, Anne, flew to Canyon de Chelly for their honeymoon, landing on the Navajo racetrack. They visited with her brother, who was doing an archaeological dig at Canyon del Muerto at the time.*

Lucky Lindy is greeted by a couple of admirers on a visit to Tucson on September 23, 1927, following his historic flight.

passengers annually to view the Grand Canyon in its Ford tri-motored planes. A year later Scenic spent $150,000 to build a new airport, called Sky Harbor, in Phoenix.

Radio Days

THE AGE OF ELECTRICITY brought entertainment into the homes and communities of Americans. Nationwide radio sales rose from less than two million in 1920 to six hundred million by 1929. By the end of the decade there were 618 radio stations nationwide, including three in Arizona.

One of the state's earliest radio operators was Barry Goldwater. He was an operator on 6BBH, an amateur experimental station that went on the air in 1921 and later became KOY. NBC began operations in 1926, followed a year later by CBS.

Arizona's first licensed commercial radio station, coming on the air on June 22, 1922, was KFAD, later changed to KTAR. (The station was later acquired by *The Arizona Republic* and the call letters were supposed to mean "Keep Taking *The Arizona Republic*.")

In 1920 two thousand youngsters attended Phoenix Union High School. That same year Arizona's first skyscraper, the Heard Building, went up, and a redwood pipeline from the Verde River to Phoenix was completed. The line never worked too well and was eventually abandoned. Some of the redwood was used to make the doors in the construction of Camelback Inn later in the decade.

Radio was still in the embryonic stage in the 1920s. By the end of the decade, fewer than 20 percent of the families in Arizona had a radio. In comparison, 90 percent of the homes had electricity and 22 percent had an electric washer. Only 2 percent had an electric refrigerator.

For those who didn't have a radio, public listening areas were set up in such places as Encanto Park in Phoenix. On September 22, 1927, some ten thousand fans gathered along Central Avenue to listen to the famous "Long Count" Heavyweight Championship boxing match between Jack Dempsey and Gene Tunney. The fight was broadcast to fifty million listeners nationwide.

A Lake of Weeds

DURING THE 1920S government surveyors went up the Gila River to find a suitable place to build a dam. They picked a site, and dam construction began. Coolidge Dam was eventually completed, and its namesake, President Calvin Coolidge, along with humorist Will Rogers, were invited to attend the opening ceremonies. The surveyors had selected the site during a wet year, and now the state was in its usual drought condition. Behind the dam where the lake was supposed to form was nothing but weeds. The president looked upon the scene and had little to say, as was characteristic. Will Rogers gazed upon the field of weeds and mused, "If that was my lake, I'd mow it." (The lake, called San Carlos, didn't fill to capacity until the 1980s.)

A Damsel in Distress

ARIZONA PLAYED A MAJOR PART in one of the great hoaxes of the decade when Aimee Semple McPherson, a popular Hollywood show business evangelist, was "kidnapped." McPherson, the daughter of a tambourine-thumping soldier in the Salvation Army, was steeped in rigid, fundamentalist Protestantism. Endowed with unique evangelistic talents and a silver tongue, and with a body even better endowed by Mother Nature, she headed for California. Soon she gained fame and fortune as a faith healer. By the mid-1920s she was running a million-dollar religious empire. "I can't stand the jingle of coins," she once told an adoring congregation. "Make it a silent offering. I can't hear paper money."

Then, on May 18, 1926, a bizarre thing happened. Newspapers around the world reported she'd died while swimming in the ocean off Santa Monica. A good swimmer, she'd just walked out into the water and disappeared. At least that was the story given by her private secretary, Emma Shaeffer.

The search continued for days, while her congregation prayed for the recovery of the body. Some saw visions of her rising from the waters and ascending into heaven. An airplane flew over Santa Monica Bay and dumped a huge load of crimson and white roses. Her disciples held a massive memorial service. Others, however, were skeptical. McPherson, it seems, had been the third party in a love triangle. She'd been named the correspondent in a divorce between Ken Ormiston and his wife, Ruth. Mr. Ormiston had also recently disappeared.

Thirty-seven days later, on June 24, the headlines of the *Arizona Daily Star* reported, "Resurrected from 'Dead' Aimee Safe." The headline added: "Kidnapped from Beach; Evangelist Held for Ransom; Staggers to Border; Relates Lurid Story of Adventure and Cruelty."

The story's dateline was from Douglas, where McPherson reappeared. The anxious world was told how she'd been chloroformed and gagged, and then made a harrowing escape with twenty miles of "delirious wandering in the Mexican desert." Dramatic news photos showed renactments of her daring escape from her captors.

Skeptics immediately wondered why her clothes didn't show signs of her terrible ordeal. Also, the buxom lady was in excellent shape after her long walk in the hot desert sun.

Soon a sympathetic press decided McPherson's three-week ordeal was really a tryst with her boyfriend, and she quickly dropped off the front pages. She was later bound over for trial on criminal conspiracy charges. Witnesses claimed she'd been sharing a cottage with Ormiston in Carmel, but the case got so muddled with conflicting testimony that the charges were eventually dismissed. The case remains shrouded in mystery. Where was Aimee Semple McPherson, and what was she doing during the thirty-seven days between her disappearance at Santa Monica and her resurrection at Douglas, Arizona?

Go West, Young Woman

DURING THE 1920S an Eastern lady named Mary Kidder married an Arizona rancher named Charlie Rak and moved to a ranch way out in the boondocks some forty miles of rough dirt road from Douglas on the Mexican border. Mrs. Rak would write two books, *Ranch Wife* and *Mountain Cattle,* telling of her memorable experiences adapting to life in the Wild West.

Her story takes a twist from the typical tales of Eastern girls coming west. She was a natural working with cattle, while her husband Charlie was better suited to the kitchen. They traded chores: He did the cooking and she tended cattle. Her visiting Eastern friends were shocked and thought her abused when they saw her out in the corral while Charlie stayed in the kitchen. They tried to emancipate Mary Kidder Rak and put her back in the house, but she would have none of it.

"Women on ranches," she wrote, "eat their share of dirt; get skinned, scraped, kicked, and dragged; worry about the market; fill out government forms—in short they have an intimate knowledge of what it takes to put anything on the table."

Once a visitor pointed out that Mary Kidder Rak needed an electric stove. Rak pointed out they had no electricity, nor other conveniences like running water or bathtubs. The insistent lady pressed on, "I have an electric refrigerator that makes cute little ice cubes," she said, "and a washing machine. I should think that more than anything else in the world you'd want electricity."

Rak looked up toward the heavens and replied, "More than anything else in the world, I want an inch of rain."

Another former Easterner, Mary Russell Ferrell Colton, who was born in 1889 in Louisville, Kentucky, could be referred to as a "keeper of the flame." Her artistic talents were recognized early. At fifteen she attended the Philadelphia School of Design for Women, where she studied under prominent artists of the day. After graduation she opened a studio and made a living full time as an artist—no easy achievement.

She married Dr. Harold S. Colton in 1912 and the newlyweds visited the nation's newest state on their honeymoon. Her love for Arizona began while visiting Flagstaff. The couple spent the next several summers around Flagstaff, also visiting the Hopi and Navajo Reservations. On these trips she made sketches for works she would complete during the winter.

In 1926 the Coltons decided to settle in Flagstaff and make Arizona their permanent residence. They built a Spanish colonial home north of town. Over the years they'd become committed to preserving the history and culture of the Colorado Plateau, and in 1928 they created the Museum of Northern Arizona. He became the first director and she, the curator.

During the next several years Colton worked tirelessly to collect, catalogue, and preserve thousands of Native American artifact as well as art and craft objects. In 1930, to promote the work of Hopi artists and create more public awareness of Native American art, she launched the Hopi Craftsman Show. At the time, only a few Hopi artists were working in silver. She encouraged them to create a design different from the Navajo and uniquely Hopi. A dozen years later she began the Navajo Craftsman Show. Over the years the shows have grown in stature, benefiting both the artists and public awareness of the arts, while the Museum of Northern Arizona has become known worldwide.

Flagstaff, 1926.

The Heard Legacy

ANOTHER GREAT ARIZONA INSTITUTION, the Heard Museum, was founded in 1928 by Maie Bartlett and Dwight B. Heard. The Museum, with its arched white walkway and hacienda ambiance, transforms the city environment into the quiet, distant past. It is one of the oldest cultural centers in the Salt River Valley.

The Heards came to Arizona from Chicago in 1895. They saw opportunity in the Salt River Valley and invested in land and banking interests. He was also president and publisher of the *Arizona Republican* newspaper. He championed such projects as the Newlands or Reclamations Act of 1902, which brought about the building of Theodore Roosevelt Dam on the Salt River. He also vigorously pushed for statehood. He was the Republican party nominee for governor in 1924, but was narrowly defeated by Governor George W. P. Hunt.

The Heards built a mansion on Central Avenue, north of McDowell Road in Phoenix. Both had a strong interest in prehistoric and modern Native American art and artifacts. The Heard Museum, a unique example of Spanish-Colonial architecture, was built in 1929 to house their collection. The Museum was doubled in size in 1969, to its current 78,000 square feet.

In 1921 the Heards also donated a barn on the property for a theater that is today the Phoenix Little Theater. The theater produced its first play that same year. During the thirties and forties and into the fifties, the Phoenix Little Theater was the city's only serious theater.

A Worldly Discovery from Flagstaff

AS THE DECADE CLOSED, Flagstaff's Lowell Observatory made news with the discovery of the planet Pluto. Wealthy author, diplomat, astronomer, mathematician, and world traveler Percival Lowell had come to Arizona in 1894. Disturbed that most observatories were located near large cities and thus hindered by artificial lighting, Lowell located

**Sections of the discovery plates that gave Clyde Tombaugh
the first-ever view of Pluto.**

the observatory on a hill west of Flagstaff, which he called Mars Hill. He
was enamored by the red planet and believed it was inhabited by intelligent life.

As early as 1902, Lowell suggested that an as yet unknown planet
existed beyond Neptune. He also calculated the location of such a planet.
It wasn't until several years after his death in 1916 that his research bore
fruit. On February 18, 1930, using a telescope especially designed for
such a project, amateur astronomer Clyde Tombaugh discovered the
planet Pluto near where Lowell said it would be. It was only the third
major planet discovered in recorded history, and the only planet discovered in America.

Lowell and others had surmised the existence of a ninth planet
because of irregularities in the motions of celestial bodies outside of
Neptune's orbit. Lowell set out to find the "trans-Neptunian planet" in
1905 by using a twenty-four-inch refractor to expose photographic plates
of the sky. Later a forty-two-inch reflector was used and the plates were
viewed through a Zeiss blink comparator, which aids in observing dif-

ferences between two images of the same portion of sky taken on differ-ent nights. The machine "blinks" the two images back and forth so the viewer can easily see shifts in movement between them.

Finally, thirteen years after Lowell's death, a thirteen-inch photographic telescope was developed, but it was Tombaugh who first laid eyes on the elusive Planet X.

Today the observatory has nine telescopes in service, including the famous Clark refractor, the pioneer telescope in the entire Southwest. Installed in 1896, the telescope has a twenty-four-inch-diameter lens and has been in continuous operation since then. It's still considered one of the finest refractors in the world.

Also among the nine telescopes is the Pluto Photographic Telescope, the thirteen-inch refractor used in the historic discovery of Pluto.

Bombing Naco

IN 1929 ANOTHER REVOLUTION broke out in Mexico. Once again, American adventurers headed south. One of them was a barnstorming pilot named Patrick Murphy. The roguish flyer offered his services to the rebels and was hired to drop bombs on *federale* trenches at the border

Naco, 1929.

town of Naco. The bombs were primitive affairs. Sometimes the bombardier was a kid who sat in the back lighting fuses with his cigarette. Other times the pilot lit the fuse and tossed it overboard. The bombs did little damage, but the spectators who came down from Bisbee to watch the fireworks enjoyed them.

For reasons only he could explain, Murphy made several bombing runs on Naco, Arizona. His bombs heavily damaged several businesses, including the Phelps Dodge store and Newton's garage. One destroyed a Dodge touring car. According to local legend, some irate citizen took a .30-06 rifle and shot down Murphy's plane. He survived the crash and was hauled off to jail in Nogales. He broke out soon after and left the area. Significantly, Murphy's bombing runs marked the only time the continental United States has been under an air attack from a foreign power.

THE ROARING TWENTIES were a happy, daring, and devil-may-care time. They began with "Professor" Woodrow Wilson, weakened by the ordeals of running a nation during wartime. The next president, Warren G. Harding, was never up to the job, had a scandal-ridden administration, and died in office. He was replaced by "Silent" Calvin Coolidge, a man who believed the business of the country was business. He napped four hours each workday. The last was Herbert Hoover. Though he was bright, he would take the blame for what followed.

The good times ended on October 24, 1929, when the stock market crashed, heralding the Great Depression of the 1930s. America would never see a decade like the twenties again. Almost overnight the country went from "anything goes," to "everything went."

HARD TIMES

"Let me assert my firm belief that the only thing we have to fear is fear itself."

—Franklin D. Roosevelt, March 4, 1933

"We are the first nation in the history of the world to go to the poor house in an automobile."

—Will Rogers, 1933

T HE GREAT DEPRESSION WAS in full bloom and hard times had fallen on the rural communities of Tempe and Mesa that Christmas of 1932. It was the height of the Christmas shopping season and local merchants were feeling the pinch. Business was slack, and it looked as if the annual Christmas parade was going to be a bust.

John McPhee, colorful editor of the *Mesa Tribune,* loved promotional schemes, but he outdid himself on this one. "Why not," he asked, "hire a parachutist to dress up in a Santa suit and jump from an airplane? He could then lead the parade through town. People will come from everywhere to see it, and while they're here they'll go Christmas shopping."

Parachuting was considered a dangerous stunt. For that matter, aviation was still a novelty. Lindbergh had flown the Atlantic only five years before. And never had Santa dropped from the sky, dangling beneath a billowing canopy.

"Splendid idea," the merchants agreed. They could almost hear the cash registers ringing like Christmas bells.

McPhee managed to find an itinerant stunt pilot who was willing to make the jump, and a deal was struck. But on the morning of the event the stunt man failed to appear. McPhee was finally able to locate his man at a local saloon, screwing up his courage on a barstool. By the time McPhee got there the man was so screwed up he couldn't get *off* the barstool.

"What now?" the worried merchants wanted to know.

"Fear not," said the irrepressible editor. "I'll borrow a department-store dummy, dress him in the Santa suit, and have the pilot toss him out of the airplane. I will then appear in another Santa suit and lead the parade through town. No one will know the difference."

An ingenious idea, the merchants agreed.

News traveled fast and hundreds of spectators gathered to witness the event. All eyes gazed anxiously skyward as the drone of the airplane's engine was heard off in the distance. Then they saw the plane circling overhead. The doorway opened and a figure in a red suit appeared. The crowd began to cheer. Then it happened. Santa seemed to leap out of the plane into the wild blue yonder. Santa appeared to be in a free-fall, and the crowd's cheery mood quickly changed to horror. Santa began to tumble end over end, down, down, down like a lead balloon. *Splat.* Santa landed facedown in the field. Mothers covered their horrified children's eyes. Fathers stared in disbelief.

Through it all, McPhee remained undaunted. He jumped out of his hiding place as if nothing had happened and proceeded to lead the parade through town. But the public wasn't buying. . . . literally and figuratively. Would-be shoppers loaded up their kids and went back to the farms. Merchants muttered unpleasantness as they stood in the doorways of their empty stores. McPhee was about as welcome around town as a coyote in a hen house.

The editor left town for a few days, hoping the event would be forgotten. It wasn't. Upon his death some thirty-six years later, the front page of the *Tribune* noted his passing with this banner: "John McPhee, The Man Who Killed Santa Claus, Dies."

Boom to Bust

THE GREAT DEPRESSION came just a decade after the First World War had left most of Europe in political and economic shambles. During the 1920s totalitarian governments were taking hold in Russia and Italy. For a time it looked as if democracy was in trouble, but by the late 1920s the economic and political situations had improved, and it seemed that even Germany was going democratic. Then came the stock market crash. Some twenty million shares of stock were dumped on the American market in the greatest economic catastrophe of all time. Americans closed their shops, lost their farms, boarded up their factories, and made runs on their banks. Many left their homes and headed West in search of a new start in some promised land.

In Arizona the Depression gave the economy a severe jolt. Mining, agriculture, and the livestock industry had boomed during the 1920s. When Eastern factories closed, the copper market collapsed. The price fell from eighteen cents a pound in 1929 to less than six cents a pound by 1932. The mines couldn't afford to stay open. Many hard-rock miners took to the hills and prospected for gold.

Citrus growers were hit hard, but cotton farmers suffered the most. People can't eat cotton. In 1928 short staple cotton was selling for nineteen cents a pound. By 1932 it hit a low of only six cents a pound. Pima long staple dropped from thirty-six cents a pound to fourteen.

Ranchers Respond

FATE DELIVERED CATTLE RANCHERS a double whammy as a severe drought hit the state with the Depression. One rancher complained it

Heading West, ca. 1930s.

was so dry that when a rain cloud finally did pass over, it let fall only a single drop of moisture . . . and four dirt clods got into a fight over it. Another said the only way he was able to grow any feed was to hire a cowboy to load up a wagon full of dirt and plant alfalfa in it. Then he'd drive the wagon around until he saw a rain cloud. He'd park the wagon under it, in hopes a few drops would fall.

Ranchers bought calves high in the spring and sold them low in the fall. Beef went from nine cents a pound to three cents. Ranchers were actually giving their cattle away. In Yavapai County, stockmen donated beef to the Salvation Army to feed the poor. In the sheep industry, the price of wool fell from thirty-six cents a pound to nine cents.

Old-timers tell of a time during the height of the Depression when a magazine writer stopped off at a hardscrabble ranch in southern Arizona. He saw an old cowman out digging post holes by the front gate. The writer gazed out across the parched ground and asked, "How do you ever make a living out here?"

The cowman wiped the sweat from his brow with a wrinkled old bandana and replied slowly. "You see that feller over there? He works for me, but I can't afford to pay him anything. So in two years the outfit will be his. Then I'll work for him 'til I get it back."

A Governor for Hard Times

ARIZONA'S DEPRESSION GOVERNOR was a crusty country doctor from Tempe named Ben Moeur. Born in Tennessee and raised in San Antonio, Texas, Moeur liked to say, "I punched cows from the time I was six years old until I was twenty." After graduating from medical school in 1896, he got married and moved to Tombstone. Later he settled in Tempe. He also had a cowboy's proclivity toward a descriptive, vivid, and profane vocabulary. Once at a party he greeted a lady, saying, "You sure look good."

She responded by saying, "I wish I could say the same for you."

He replied, "You could if you were as big a liar as me."

Despite his coarse, gruff manner, he had a heart of gold and was a great humanitarian who never refused to help those in need. During construction of Roosevelt Dam he had himself transported across Salt River Canyon in a cement bucket attached to a cable to aid an injured worker. While he was governor, Moeur spent his lunch hour in the rotunda of the capitol building doctoring indigent folks for free. At Christmas, when he knew clients were too poor to pay their doctor bills, he'd send a Christmas card with these words inscribed: "Paid in full." This writer's family received one of those cards from the good doctor.

To War for Water

HEADLINES 1930

✳ *On November 11, 1930,* The Arizona Republican *became* The Arizona Republic. *By 1930 the population of the state was over 435,000 and Phoenix had a population of nearly 50,000. It had 161 miles of streets, of which 77 were paved. Another pipeline hauling water from the Verde was completed. This time they used concrete, and it's still in use.*

IT WAS DURING Governor Moeur's tenure that Arizona engaged in a naval war with California. It all began when the state's water-guzzling neighbor to the west pulled enough political strings to have a dam built on the Colorado River at Parker. California, which contributed no water to the river, was about to take a lion's share. Moeur mobilized the National Guard and sent them to the Arizona shore, where they set up machine gun emplacements. When the construction workers saw guns aimed in their direction, they shut down the job.

One evening some guardsmen manned a couple of steamboats owned by a local, Nellie Bush, to reconnoiter the other side. Bush was commissioned "Admiral of the Arizona Navy" for allowing her boats to be commandeered for active duty. Murphy's Law came into play, however, and the recon boats got hung up in some cables. Their worst nightmare came true: The Arizona Navy had to be rescued by Californians. The incident made the national newspapers and caused some red faces in the state. The Supreme Court got into the act and ordered Governor Moeur to "bring the troops home."

A New Deal for Arizona

ROOSEVELT S NEW DEAL tried a myriad of programs to jump-start the economy. One of the successful programs in Arizona was the CCC or

PRICE INDEX

During the years 1932 to 1934, prices were relatively low. A used 1929 Ford cost only $57. A new Pontiac coupe, $585. A woman's wool dress cost $1.95 and a man's suit, $10.50. A Stetson hat would set you back $5. A shave cost a dime, and a haircut, 20 cents. A lady's hair bob or a children's Buster Brown cost 30 cents. At the local restaurant a sirloin steak dinner cost a quarter; a hamburger steak, 15 cents; and ham and eggs, 20 cents.

Annual earnings during that time: Coal miners earned $723 a year; farm hands, $216; construction workers, $907; teachers, $1,227; doctors, $3,382; and lawyers, $4,218.

Babe Ruth won a salary dispute with the Yankees and was earning $80,000 a year. When a writer mentioned he was being paid more than President Hoover, the Babe remarked, "I'm having a better year than he is."

Civilian Conservation Corps.

Civilian Conservation Corps. Beginning in 1933, it promoted a nationwide program of conservation and at the same time offered vocational training to young men. The men were organized in quasi-military groups and, although nobody knew it at the time, the CCC provided training that would better prepare these men for service in the next decade. They were paid thirty dollars a month, most of which was sent home to dependents or parents. Like the military, they were clothed, fed, sheltered, educated, and given medical care.

By 1936 there were more than forty CCC camps in Arizona and some nine thousand corpsmen at work. They built sturdy picnic facilities at South Mountain Park in Phoenix that are still in use today. They constructed flood retention dams, built pathways in Colossal Cave (a tourist attraction near Tucson), and lined irrigation canals with cement. They reseeded overgrazed land with native grasses and built a trail down into the Grand Canyon. The trail-building corpsmen even performed some yeoman's duty: When the ranger's wife, who was living at Phantom Ranch in the bottom of the Canyon, complained about missing her piano, the young men hauled it down the trail. They were handsomely rewarded for their efforts when she entertained them with piano concerts during evening hours.

Cowboy Kennedy

IN THE SUMMER OF 1936, a couple of unlikely cowhands worked on the J-6 ranch near Benson. The two oldest Kennedy brothers, Joseph and

John, came out west to be cowboys. Actually, John was having health problems and the family believed ranch work would toughen him up. The boys herded livestock and mended fences. They also constructed an adobe room with a Mexican-style fireplace in one corner. According to their boss, John Speiden, the two boys were "willing and hard workers." By the time the boys left for Massachusetts, Speiden pronounced them "leather-tough and tanned."

Many years later Speiden attended a dinner in Washington with President Kennedy and told him, "When your presidency is over, I want you to know that your old job as a cowboy is still waiting for you." Kennedy grinned and replied he'd keep that offer in mind.

John F. Kennedy would return to Arizona after the war to do some rehabilitation in the hot, therapeutic waters at Castle Hot Springs. The old resort was a rehab center for pilots in 1944 and 1945. He also spent some time "recuperating" with the young ladies around the swimming pool at Camelback Inn. Kennedy spoke with genuine fondness for the state when recalling the people he'd met during his visits.

Joe and John (on fence, left to right) at the J-6 Ranch near Benson, 1936.

Hollywood Comes to Arizona

THE MOVIES WERE A GREAT ESCAPE during the Depression. The top box-office draw was precocious little Shirley Temple; she was earning a salary of three hundred thousand dollars, while her studio made an astounding five million annually.

Contrast that to the economy of the Navajo Nation in northern Arizona. Life for the Navajo had always been tough. Making a living in the *mal país,* or badlands, was never easy, even before the Great Depression.

Harry and Mike Goulding opened a trading post on the Arizona-Utah border in 1923. The young couple took an active interest in the welfare of the Navajo. They not only purchased wool blankets and the arts and crafts of the natives but also settled disputes between families and clans and acted as a liaison, handling paperwork between the Navajo and the federal government.

During the Depression, Harry learned Hollywood was looking for spectacular vistas to film Western movies. He loaded up his old car with some of photographer Josef Muench's black-and-white photos of Monument Valley and headed for Tinsel Town. His mission was to show the photos to famed director John Ford, but Ford's secretary gave him the brush-off when she learned he had no appointment. Undaunted, he rolled a Navajo blanket out on the floor and informed her he would camp out in her office until Mr. Ford was available.

She brought out an assistant director to remove him from the premises, but as Goulding was being hustled out the door he flash-carded Muench's photos in the assistant's face. The spectacular vistas caught his eye, and in a matter of moments they were spread out on the floor again. This time, John Ford himself was gazing with awe. The rest is history.

Ford gave Goulding carte blanche to go back to Monument Valley and set up facilities for a movie set. Ford was planning to film the old Ernest Haycox novel, *Stage to Lordsburg* under the name *Stagecoach,* and Monument Valley was to be the location. It would be the first major film for a young man named John Wayne.

In that film Navajo people were hired to portray a war party of Apaches. During the next couple of decades Ford returned again and again to make films. The Navajos played Comanches, Cheyennes, and Navajos in *Wagonmaster,* a film that starred Ben Johnson, Joanne Dru, and Harry Carey, Jr.

These films and others that followed made Monument Valley one of the world's most recognizable locations and tourism a major industry, all starting with the tireless efforts of the Gouldings.

DURING THE LATE 1920S, Bob Nolan was a star athlete at Tucson High School. In 1927 he began hopping freight trains and exploring the West. His love for music and talent for writing drew him to California, and in 1931 he teamed up with another drifter from Ohio, Leonard Slye, forming the Rocky Mountaineers. Nolan's first hit song, "Tumbling Tumbleweeds," came in 1934. The song was inspired one day when Nolan was gazing out his window and noticed some leaves blowing down the street. He wrote the words to a song called "Tumbling Leaves." Later, "tumbleweeds" was substituted for "leaves." Today the song is considered one of the great all-time classics in Western music.

Nolan, Leonard Slye, Tim Spenser, and Hugh and Karl Farr formed the legendary Sons of the Pioneers. "Tumbling Tumbleweeds" was the group's theme song. Len Slye changed his name to Dick Weston before finally going into the movies and calling himself Roy Rogers. After Rogers became a movie star with Republic Pictures, the group appeared in most of his films.

AMERICA'S FIRST WOMAN TO SERVE IN CONGRESS

✸ *The election of 1933 produced a first for the state. When Congressman Lewis Douglas resigned his seat to become Roosevelt's Director of the Budget, Isabella Selmes Greenway took his place. In a special election, Greenway, the widow of former Rough Rider and copper magnate John C. Greenway, was elected to Congress. A child-hood friend and bridesmaid of First Lady Eleanor Roosevelt, Greenway was the first woman from Arizona to serve in Congress.*

While he was still a student at Tucson High School, Bob Nolan wrote a poem called "Cool Water." It was later recorded as a song by the Sons of the Pioneers, and in a survey conducted in 1951 it was found to be the "best-known song of the American West." Nolan, who has been credited with creating the sound and style of Western harmony singing, died in 1980. After cremation, according to his last wishes, Bob Nolan's ashes were scattered across the Nevada desert.

Keeping Cool

IT'S BEEN SAID that necessity is the mother of invention, and the desert heat produced more than one inventor of the "swamp cooler." Nobody knows for certain who was the first to invent the evaporative cooler, but A. J. Eddy of Yuma and Oscar Palmer of Phoenix are among those who've been credited. The contraption's popularity spread quickly, and soon Phoenix was known as the "Cooler Capital of the World," producing 40 percent of all evaporative coolers sold in the world.

In 1929 the Westward Ho Hotel became the first building to have air conditioning in Arizona. It was soon followed by the Orpheum and Fox Theaters in downtown Phoenix. In addition to swimming pools like Riverside Park, movie theaters became a good place to escape the summer heat. (It was not until the 1950s that refrigerated air conditioning became affordable in homes.)

Cops and Robbers

THE ARIZONA HIGHWAY PATROL, forerunner of the Department of Public Safety, was created by the legislature in 1931. It was the first state-wide police force. Up until this time, county peace officers couldn't cross the county line in pursuit of criminals. (It wasn't the first time Arizona had a law-enforcement agency that could cross county lines. From 1901 to 1909 the Arizona Rangers were able to go anywhere in the territory in pursuit of lawbreakers. Occasionally they even crossed into Mexico to catch a badman.)

The new Highway Patrol originally provided for a superintendent and one patrolman in each county. By 1938 the number had increased to forty-two patrolmen statewide. By this time there were 147,000 vehicles registered in the state. The agency's primary mission at the offset was to increase the registration of vehicles and licensing of drivers. Later, patrolmen were responsible for the enforcement of traffic laws on the state's new highways.

Arizona made the national crime news more than once during the thirties. Tucson was a sleepy desert town with a population of a little over thirty thousand on January 21, 1934. Gangsters on the run considered it a quiet place out in the boondocks with a police force made up of a bunch of rubes. It seemed to be a perfect place for a band of midwestern desperadoes to lie low for awhile.

One such band was staying in the Congress Hotel that night when the building caught fire. Firemen tried to evacuate the building, but certain guests were insistent about taking along their baggage. They gave the firemen some hassle, which aroused suspicions. The bags seemed unusually heavy. Three days later a fireman was reading *True Detective* magazine at the firehouse and recognized Russell Clark, a member of the notorious John Dillinger gang, as one of the men in the Congress Hotel the night of the fire.

About that same time, in a Tucson bar, a couple of men were boasting to the customers about how easy it was to rob banks. The two were recognized by locals as "Fat Charlie" Markley and "Crazy Harry" Pierpoint. With them was Opal Love, a buxom redhead known as "The Mack Truck."

Tucson police were alerted, and they knew trouble was at hand. These guys were dangerous killers, especially Pierpoint, who wouldn't be taken without a fight. Innocent people might get hurt. So they came up with a plan to take the gang without firing a shot.

Fat Charlie Markley was found at a radio repair shop. Officers walked up and notified him that cars with out-of-state license plates had to come into the station for a routine check of the papers. He obligingly went to the station, where he was quickly arrested.

Next the lawmen picked up Clark and Opal Love at a rented house at 927 North Second Avenue. Clark started to resist, but lawman Frank Eyman slammed his pistol up beside the outlaw's head. Clark was escorted to the station without any further resistance.

John Dillinger in his heyday as Public Enemy Number One.

Crazy Harry Pierpoint was spotted driving and was asked to pull over for a routine check to clear the papers on his automobile. He also agreed to go to the station and even allowed Eyman to ride in the back seat. Eyman rode with his pistol concealed between his knees, but there was no trouble. As they walked into the station, Pierpoint recognized the stash of the gang's machine guns. He started to resist but was overwhelmed and disarmed by officers. Among his weapons was a hideout gun on a string down his back.

Where was Dillinger? All this time he was holed up in the Close-Inn Tourist Court on South Sixth Avenue with his moll, pretty Evelyn Frechette. Believing Dillinger would eventually show, police kept a stake-out at the house on Second Avenue. When Dillinger appeared, Frank Eyman walked up and quietly told him he was under arrest. Dillinger's only comment was, "Well, I'll be damned."

A bunch of small-town cops had nabbed the country's most notorious gang without firing a shot. It was a great moment for the Tucson Police Department.

Dillinger and his friends were returned to jail in Indiana. Thirty-one days later Dillinger broke jail and disappeared. He was reportedly seen in dozens of places at the same time. Then, on July 27, 1934, he died in a hail of bullets outside the Biograph Theater in Chicago, betrayed by the mysterious "Lady in Red." FBI agent Melvin Purvis and sixteen assistants brought an end to Public Enemy Number One. Surprisingly, Dillinger's great crime spree had lasted just fourteen months.

Tucson lawman Frank Eyman went on to have a great career in law enforcement, capping his career as warden of the state prison at Florence.

The Only Woman to Hang in Arizona

ONE OF THE MOST BIZARRE CRIMES of the decade involved a "physically challenged" woman named Eva Dugan. In late December 1926, she hired out to work as a housekeeper for Tucson rancher Andy Mathis. Two weeks later he hired a young man named Jack as a handyman around the place. The day of Jack's arrival was the last day Mathis was seen alive. Dugan told the neighbors Mathis had gone to California for awhile and had authorized her to sell some of his livestock and a Dodge automobile. Then she and Jack took off for Nogales.

Pima County Sheriff Jimmy McDonald was called out to investigate. He found Mathis's cash box missing and his hearing trumpet stashed in a pot-bellied stove. Suspecting foul play, McDonald put out an all-points bulletin across the country. He learned that Dugan had sold the car in Amarillo, Texas, for six hundred dollars under the name Mrs. Eva Mathis. Then she and Jack headed for Kansas City. After that, Jack was never seen again. Dugan was apprehended in New York and extradited back to Arizona on a theft charge.

While she was doing time on the theft charge, someone camping on the Mathis ranch was setting a tent pole when he discovered a shallow grave. The body was identified as Mathis, and Dugan was charged with murder.

At her trial Dugan claimed Jack accidentally killed Mathis during a fight. The jury didn't believe her, and neither did the state Supreme Court, claiming that by her own testimony she was "immoral, profane, and intemperate. She had been married five times, the bonds being severed four times by death and once by divorce." It's never been determined whether Eva Dugan had anything to do with her previous husbands' deaths.

Dugan was hanged on February 21, 1930, at the state prison at Florence. She is the only woman ever put to death in the state of Arizona. At her hanging the balance weights were adjusted improperly, and because of her weight (she was what we politely call today "obesity-challenged"), her head snapped off as she dropped through the trap.

In 1933 Arizona voters chose the lethal gas chamber as a means of execution over hanging. (Today lethal injection is the most common type of legal execution in Arizona.)

The Trunk Murderess

ARIZONA'S MOST SENSATIONAL CRIME during the decade occurred in Phoenix when three young women got into a fight that resulted in the deaths of two of them. On the evening of October 16, 1931, Winnie Ruth Judd and two friends, Anne Le Roi and Hedvig "Sammy" Samuelson got into an argument and began fighting. In a rage, Le Roi grabbed an ironing board and began beating Winnie Ruth over the head, at the same time shouting to Samuelson, "Kill her." Samuelson came at Winnie Ruth with a gun, and as the two grappled, the gun went off, killing Samuelson.

Winnie Ruth then took the gun and fired a fatal round into Le Roi. During the melee, Winnie Ruth also took a bullet in the left hand. In a panic, she returned to her apartment, where she was supposed to meet a friend, Jack Halloran.

Halloran, age forty-four, was a handsome ladies' man, well known around town. He was well connected and a member of the Phoenix Country Club. Although married with a family, he socialized often with Winnie Ruth and her friends.

Winnie Ruth, a pretty redhead, was also married. Her husband, Dr. William Judd, was several years older than she. He was addicted to drugs and away a lot, leaving his young wife alone. He was in California the night of the killings.

Anne Le Roi was attractive and twice divorced. Sammy Samuelson was slender and pretty. She and Le Roi lived together. They entertained men, but rumors persisted the two were in a lesbian relationship. It those days a gay relationship was taboo. It's been said the fight that night began when Winnie Ruth threatened to expose Samuelson and Le Roi to their employers at the Grunow Clinic, where they all worked.

Phoenix was a city of about 48,000 in 1931, and when Halloran learned of the killings, he feared the publicity might be damaging to him. He suggested they put the two bodies in trunks and quietly dispose of them in the desert. According to later testimony, a Dr. Charles Brown was called to cut Samuelson's body so she'd fit in the trunk.

Winnie Ruth planned to go to Los Angeles to see her husband and have the bullet wound taken care of. Halloran suggested she take the trunks with her. She foolishly agreed. In shock from the gunshot wound and the horrible experience, she was obviously not thinking clearly. By the time the train arrived in Los Angeles, blood was seeping from the trunks and the stench was horrible. As people began to eye the trunks suspiciously, Winnie Ruth slipped away from the train station, hiding out for three days before turning herself in to the authorities. By this time the press had sensationalized the case. When she was returned to Phoenix in a caravan, some twenty thousand people lined the streets to catch a glimpse of the "Trunk Murderess," and "Tiger Woman."

The authorities decided Winnie Ruth acted alone in the murder of her two friends. The prosecution went for murder one, claiming Winnie Ruth murdered the two girls in their beds while they slept. However, there were no blood stains on the walls and the mattresses were mysteriously missing. One was later recovered in the desert a couple miles away. No one bothered to explain how it got there, since the defendant didn't know how to drive. It's also worth noting that Winnie Ruth, a frail woman, couldn't have lifted Le Roi, who weighed 140 pounds, and put her in a trunk. There were no scrape marks on the floor, so she would have had to carry the trunk out of the house, something she couldn't have done. Curiously, she was only tried for the murder of Le Roi, who wasn't mutilated, yet it was Samuelson's mutilated body that was discussed during the trial. Samuelson's death never came to trial. Before he could testify, Dr. Brown conveniently died of a heart attack.

There was something else strange about the case: Samuelson died from a .25-caliber gunshot wound, while Anne was fatally wounded with a .32 bullet.

At the trial, neither Winnie Ruth nor Halloran was called to testify. The jury should have been given an option of self-defense but wasn't.

On February 24, 1932, Winnie Ruth Judd was found guilty and sentenced to hang.

Dr. William Judd capitalized on his wife's plight by selling stories to magazines for thousands of dollars each. While on death row, just hours before she was to hang, Winnie Ruth was declared insane. She was told to sit tight for a couple of years until things quieted down and she would then go free. By 1939 her patience ran out and she began her legendary escapes from the state hospital.

In 1952 another grand jury agreed she didn't kill in cold blood and that all she needed to be set free was a sanity hearing. She didn't get one, so she continued to escape for a few days of freedom at a time. Newspapers had only to say on their banners, "Winnie Ruth is Gone Again," and everybody knew. To Arizonans, she became a harmless folk hero.

At the asylum she was very popular with both workers and inmates. She had a beauty parlor and helped counsel inmates. Many years later it would be learned she was given a key to the front door by one of the nurses.

On October 8, 1962, she escaped with the help of a relative and went to California, where she lived for the next seven years before being caught and brought back to the state hospital.

After much publicity, she was given another hearing in 1971 and told she would be released with one stipulation: She couldn't tell her story. On December 22, 1971, Winnie Ruth Judd was free at last.

She'd spent thirty-nine years of her life incarcerated for the crime. Most experts agree that today she probably would have been tried for manslaughter and served a year or two behind bars. (More than sixty years after the killings, her controversial story generated considerable interest again, when author Jana Bombersbach wrote an excellent book, *The Trunk Murderess: Winnie Ruth Judd.*)

The End of a Decade

BY 1939 THE DECADE OF HARD TIMES was winding down. Postage stamps cost three cents; a pound loaf of bread cost eight cents; a quart of milk was twelve cents; gas sold for nineteen cents a gallon; the average cost of a house was about $6,400; and the minimum wage was thirty cents an hour.

In the movies of 1939, Hattie McDaniel won an Academy Award for Best Supporting Actress for *Gone With the Wind,* the first African-American to win an Oscar. Best picture was also *Gone With the Wind.* Another film classic, *The Wizard of Oz* had its premiere. That same year, at a cost of a half-million dollars, a movie-set studio was built west of Tucson and called, appropriately enough, Old Tucson. The first movie made in the adobe village reminiscent of 1860s Arizona was called *Arizona* and starred Jean Arthur and William Holden.

Wilbur Shaw won the Indianapolis 500 with a speed of 155 miles per hour. On June 2, the immortal Iron Man, Lou Gehrig, took himself out of the New York Yankee lineup after playing in 2,130 consecutive games. The Yankee captain's endurance record would stand for nearly sixty years.

**Old Tucson, 1939 set for the movie *Arizona*
starring Jean Arthur and William Holden.**

That year Albert Einstein wrote Franklin D. Roosevelt, suggesting an atomic bomb was feasible. And, most ominous, on September 1, 1939, shortly after signing a nonaggression pact with Russia, Adolph Hitler's armies invaded Poland. Two days later France and England declared war on Germany. It was the war, rather than economic measures, that would pull the world out of an economic abyss. Arizona, America, and the world would be changed forever. For the state, it was the ushering in of what would be called Modern Arizona.

Camping in the mountains in 1938 was a far cry from what it is today.

HEROES, BASEBALL, AND A NEW INDUSTRY

"Yesterday, December 7, 1941, a date which will live in infamy. . . ."

—Franklin D. Roosevelt in his declaration of war message to Congress on December 8, 1941

S THE FORTIES BEGAN, a storm was gathering in Europe and Asia. Hitler had clamped a tight iron fist around Europe, and Japan was continuing the rape of China. In America, theater-goers were lining up to see *Gone With the Wind,* and on juke-boxes everywhere could be heard the baby-talk voice of Wee Bonnie Baker singing "Oh Johnny, Oh Johnny, Oh!"

The 1940s also marked the early stages of the teenage revolution. Youngsters began asserting themselves with wild fashions. Bobby-soxers found high fashion in mismatching shoes and socks. Another brief fad was the broad, baggy "zoot suits." Boys decked themselves out with oversized, pegged-leg trousers, pulled up to the chest and held there by suspenders. The outfit was topped off with a wide-brimmed fedora hat, extra-long watch chain, and bow tie.

Tough, durable plastic 45 rpm records were fast replacing the brittle, easily broken 78s. The jukebox industry blossomed, and the record industry boomed as discretionary money increased with the economic recovery.

Boys decorated their rooms with scantily clad pinups of Petty Girls (named for an artist who drew pinups) and pilfered road signs. The most popular pinups were Betty Grable and Rita Hayworth. That famous picture showing the beautiful backside of Ms. Grable with her head turned over her shoulder was actually shot that way because she was pregnant at the time.

Just before 8:00 A.M. on that fateful Sunday morning of December 7, 1941, the skies over Pearl Harbor were suddenly filled with the scream-ing sounds of Japanese warplanes. Minutes later some two hundred fighters, dive bombers, and torpedo planes attacked the airfields and the U.S. Pacific Fleet anchored nearby. By 9:45, in less than two hours, the

Japanese had crippled the main force of the U.S. fleet, sinking or badly damaging seven battleships, including the USS *Arizona,* three cruisers, and two destroyers. Air defenses had been wiped out, with most of the aircraft destroyed before they could get off the ground. When the smoke cleared, 2,403 sailors, marines, soldiers, and civilians were dead, and another 1,178 had been wounded.

The USS *Arizona* was the worst hit. Nearly half of those killed at Pearl Harbor were lost when the giant battleship was struck by two torpedoes and seven bombs. A 1,500-pound bomb tore through the deck and hit near the forward magazine, blowing off a 110-foot section of the bow. In a huge display of fireworks, the ship exploded and sank in minutes, taking with her 1,102 sailors who were trapped below deck. Their bodies remain entombed in the waters of Pearl Harbor to this day. Some 1,400 of the crew were on board that fateful morning, and of those, 1,177 were killed. Nine Arizonans were members of the crew, and all but one went down with the ship.

Three aircraft carriers, the *Lexington, Saratoga,* and *Enterprise,* were out to sea on that fateful morning and escaped destruction. These carriers would play an important role in the months to come. Meanwhile, in the U.S., the most massive shipbuilding and arms manufacture in history was launched.

The attack on Pearl Harbor and those who were derelict in their duty has been cussed and discussed by history buffs and military historians. It's worth noting however, that from 1931 on every graduating class at Japan's naval academy had the same exam question: "How would you carry out a surprise attack on Pearl Harbor?"

The sneak attack was a brilliant success in the short run. By nearly destroying the U.S. Pacific fleet, Japan was able to complete its Asian conquests. And yet the Japanese attack on Pearl Harbor was a serious strategic miscalculation. Americans went from a state of shock to one of anger and vengeance. The isolationism that divided them evaporated overnight, and they collectively rolled up their sleeves and prepared for war. Admiral Isoroku Yamamoto, who led the attack on Pearl Harbor, said prophetically, "I fear we have awakened a sleeping giant."

The Training Fields of Arizona

THE DRY, HOT, INHOSPITABLE DESERTS of western Arizona were an ideal place to train soldiers for the invasion of North Africa. The track marks from General George Patton's tanks are still visible on the western deserts. Soldiers stationed at Camp Hyder claimed the beverages at the post exchange were so hot that whenever a soldier got a bottle of beer under a hundred degrees it was considered a "cold one."

Army experts found more perfect flying weather in Arizona than anywhere else in the U.S., and in June 1941, they began training pilots in an intensive ten-week course. Training along with the British and Americans were Chinese pilots. The training director for the Chinese flyers was Captain Christy Mathewson, son of the legendary New York Giants pitcher.

During the war Luke Field (named for WWI ace Frank Luke, Jr.) was the largest single-engine flying school in the U.S. Williams Field, named for Arizona-born First Lieutenant Charles Williams (a flyer lost when his plane crashed into the sea off the coast of Hawaii in 1927), came into existence about the same time as Luke Field. Its mission was to train bomber pilots. After the war, Williams Air Force Base pilots became the first to fly the F-80 Shooting Star jet combat fighter.

Unlike Luke and Williams Fields, Thunderbird Field at Glendale was privately owned by Southwest Airways. Its operations, however, were under the supervision of the U.S. Army, and its mission was the training of British and Chinese pilots. Most of these pilots had never been up in a plane. Eventually, Southwest Airways would also train airmen at Thunderbird No. 2 at Scottsdale and Falcon Field at Mesa.

Young British cadets who came all the way to Mesa's Falcon Field from cold England had quite a shock when they arrived by train at Union Station in Phoenix. They were still wearing their heavy woolen uniforms. Many had never even driven an automobile, much less flown an airplane.

In 1940 Davis-Monthan Airport became a military airfield, the Army Air Forces' Heavy Bombardment Base. Flying B-24 Liberators twenty-four hours a day, seven days a week, Davis-Monthan graduated the skilled ten-man precision bombing crews that eventually rained bombs upon German targets.

During the war, other pilot training fields were located from Kingman, Williams, St. Johns, Cottonwood, and Prescott in the north, to Nogales, Yuma, Marana, and Douglas in the south. By the war's end more than two hundred thousand American, British, and Chinese airmen had earned their wings over the skies of Arizona.

Willie and Joe Go to War

A COUPLE OF CARTOON CHARACTERS named Willie and Joe showed America the war as seen through the eyes of the muddy, foot-slogging GI. Their creator was a puckish cartoonist named Bill Mauldin, who blended humor with misery in depicting the war-weary, grizzled soldiers making it through combat one day at a time.

Mauldin graduated from Phoenix Union High School, where he sketched for the student newspaper. When war came, he enlisted in the Arizona National Guard and eventually wound up in Sicily. Firing irreverent broadsides at every aspect of army life, Mauldin himself had spent sixty-four days out of his first four months in the army doing punitive KP duty. He became the unofficial spokesman for all GIs. His sardonic, grim dogfaces with their dented helmets, scruffy beards, and weary eyes pretty well summed up the ambiance of the foot soldier's war. Afterward, he was decorated and called the "best-known and most popular" soldier in the Mediterranean Theater. He won the Pulitzer Prize in 1945.

Up Front, the title of his cartoon

Up Front, by Bill Mauldin.

series, was made into a movie in the late 1940s. Later, Mauldin became a celebrated political cartoonist, winning a second Pulitzer Prize in 1959.

Internment

ON THE DARKER SIDE of the home front, thousands of Japanese Americans were rounded up and relocated into internment camps. Poston, a relocation center on the Colorado River near Parker, was the third largest city in Arizona during the war. In 1942 the War Department authorized the relocation of Japanese-Americans from military installations in California. A line was drawn that extended into Arizona along U.S. Highway 60 through Phoenix and Globe. This created a strange situation in the Phoenix area, for it meant Japanese-Americans living on the north side of Grand Avenue were sent to relocation centers, while those who lived on the south side weren't. At the time there were some six hundred Japanese-Americans living in the state, most of whom weren't affected by this order.

For some young Japanese, the only way out of the camps was to volunteer for the military. Ironically, the 442nd Regimental Combat Team, the most decorated unit in the war, was made up of Japanese-Americans.

The Crazy Boatmen of Arizona

THE LARGEST PRISONER-OF-WAR ESCAPE inside the United States occurred at Papago Park during the 1944 Christmas holidays. Located just east of Phoenix, the camp housed as many as four thousand captives, most of whom were hard-core Nazi sailors, sent to the Arizona desert to get them as far away from water as possible.

Under the leadership of U-Boat skipper Captain Jürgen Wattenberg they proposed building a *faustball* (volleyball court). This was actually a ruse to dispose of the displaced dirt from an escape tunnel. Over a period of three months, they diligently dug down some fourteen feet through the tough, clay-like caliche, then another one hundred eighty feet to the Salt River Project's Crosscut Canal.

Three of the prisoners built a small boat, which they planned to float down the river to Yuma, where they could make arrangements to go on to Mexico. The maps they'd studied showed blue lines, which usually designate rivers. The Germans didn't realize that Arizona's rivers were usually dry.

On December 23, 1944, while other prisoners threw a loud party as a diversion, twenty-five German prisoners, including Captain Wattenberg, crawled through the tunnel and made their escape. The three prisoners with the boat found the river they sought, but true to form, it was a dry bed. To this day in Germany they are known as the "Crazy Boatmen of Arizona."

The others, with the exception of Captain Wattenberg, were soon captured. Some found prison life easier than hiking the desert to the Mexican border. One surrendered to a housewife who was hanging out laundry on her clothesline.

Captain Wattenberg spent the winter and spring hiding in the mountains north of the elegant Biltmore Resort, giving him claim to being the first German winter visitor. Then one January day he walked into Phoenix, and in a heavy German accent, asked a gas station attendant for directions to the train station. That did him in. Thus closed the chapter on the "great escape."

War Heroes

DURING THE POSTWAR YEARS heroes were easy to find. Throughout the last half of the twentieth century, the great majority of political, civic, and corporate leaders who led this nation to economic prosperity and victory in the Cold War were veterans who, as young men, won their spurs in the service of their country.

Joe Foss, today a resident of Arizona, was a one-man wrecking crew in the air during the battle for Guadalcanal in 1942, when he shot five Japanese planes in one day. The Marine ace shot down a total of twenty-six Japanese planes in the war. After the war he was elected governor of South Dakota, and after that, first president of the American Football

League. He later hosted a national television outdoor show before retiring to Arizona.

The most decorated soldier in the war was Army Lieutenant Audie Murphy, a skinny kid from Texas. He won a host of medals, including the Congressional Medal of Honor. When his picture graced the cover of *Life* magazine, Hollywood talent scouts signed him up, and soon he was a movie star. Murphy served under the command of a man destined to become one of Arizona's most influential politicians, Burton Barr.

Major Barr, a resourceful officer himself, won a couple of Silver Stars for bravery. In 1951 Barr moved to Arizona and continued to serve in the Army reserve. In 1964 he entered state politics and quickly rose to a House leadership role. He was called the state's "most powerful back-slapper, arm-twister, and policy-shaper." He was characterized by a quick and self-deprecating wit and waggling eyebrows. He was colorful, funny, and tough. In the words of *Arizona Republic* reporter Keven Ann Willey, he "could charm the skin off a snake." (Barr made an unsuccessful bid in the gubernatorial race in 1986, but was upset by Evan Mecham. Barr died in January, 1997.)

One Arizonan who went to war without a rifle was popular radio personality Howard Pyle, the son of a Wyoming minister. Pyle, who became well-known for his Easter Sunrise Services at the Grand Canyon and later became governor, was sent to the Pacific theater to interview Arizonans for the folks back home.

More than thirty thousand Arizonans served in the military during World War II and more than sixteen hundred gave their lives for their country. Among those Arizonans was twenty-one-year-old Grant Turley. Flying a P-47 Thunderbolt, he was Arizona's first World War II ace. A fearless flyer, Turley once attacked a formation of ten German fighters by himself. He managed to down two before escaping. For that, he was awarded the Silver Star. He flew at least seventy missions out of England as fighter cover for the B-17 bombers, including the first air raid on Berlin. He shot down nine German planes before he was killed on March 6, 1944.

Grant Turley was raised on a ranch between Heber and Show Low and was the younger brother of Stan Turley, who would later serve in the state legislature as Speaker of the House and President of the Senate. On the side of Grant's Thunderbolt was a painting of the family ranch crest: a cow's head over a pattern of Turley family brands.

Arizona's greatest war hero was Army Pfc. Sylvestre Herrera. A native of Phoenix, he was the only Arizonan to win the Congressional Medal of Honor in World War II. On March 15, 1945, with his outfit pinned down by German machine guns and protected by mine fields, Herrera twice mounted one-man charges on the machine-gun nests. In his first assault he captured eight Germans. On his second a mine blew off his feet. Still he continued to fight, pinning down the German troops until his comrades were able to mount an attack. For this act of bravery, President Harry S. Truman pinned on his chest the nation's highest honor.

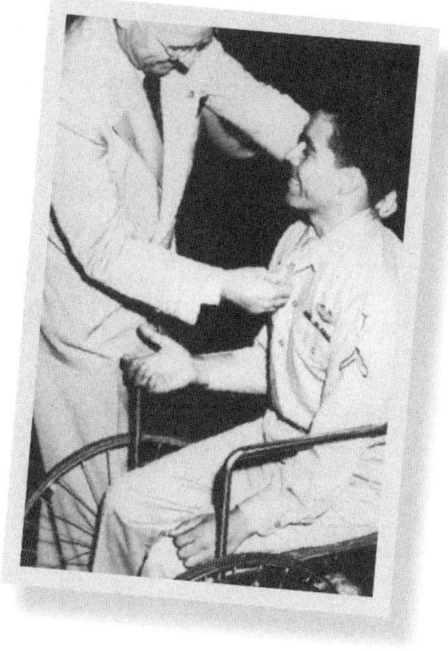

Sylvestre Herrera receiving the Congressional Medal of Honor from President Harry S. Truman, 1945.

When William Faulkner wrote, "You show me a hero and I'll write you a tragedy," he could have been referring to a Pima Indian from Bapchule, Arizona, named Ira Hamilton Hayes. Hayes was one of the small group of Marines who fought their way to the top of Mt. Suribachi, Iwo Jima, in February 1945. The photo turned out to be one of the most famous ever taken in battle, and Hayes became a national hero. After the flag-raising the battle raged on another thirty-one days and was the bloodiest single battle in the Pacific theater. Of the two hundred fifty men in Hayes' company, only twenty-seven survived. Three of the six flag-raisers, including twenty-two-year-old Ira Hayes, came down that hill alive.

Ira Hayes was from Bapchule, a Pima Indian village on the banks of the Gila River. He attended Phoenix Indian School, where he starred in

Ira Hayes.

Mt. Suribachi, Iwo Jima. Ira Hayes is the marine with the rifle slung over his shoulder.

baseball and football. In the Marines, he was a qualified paratrooper and had won two bronze stars for gallantry at Vella Lavella and Bougainville.

On his return home, Hayes was wined and dined, but he had a tough time dealing with his new-found celebrity status. Hayes requested that he be returned to combat and rejoined his outfit fighting in the Pacific. After the war he was an even bigger celebrity. He sought refuge on the Pima Indian Reservation but found no inner peace. Tragically, he died in 1955, at the age of thirty-two. He was given a hero's burial at Arlington National Cemetery. In later years, Hayes was remembered in film and song. *The Outsider,* starring Tony Curtis as Hayes, told his tragic story. Peter La Farge wrote a song recorded by Johnny Cash called "The Legend of Ira Hayes."

Unsung Heroes

AMONG THE MOST UNSUNG HEROES of the war were the Navajo Code Talkers who served in the Marines. They numbered about fifteen hundred, and their deeds and exploits fooling the Japanese with their ingenious code saved countless American lives in the Pacific campaigns.

Japanese intelligence officers, schooled in America, spoke fluent English and knew things American, from Betty Grable's measurements to Joe DiMaggio's batting average. They intercepted messages and created chaos on American radios until the Navajos arrived. Recruited on the reservation and trained at Camp Pendleton, California, the Code Talkers designed a code using the Navajo language that completely confused and confounded the Japanese. The code was so hush-hush that the Navajos were sworn to secrecy even after the war and therefore were never accorded the honor they so richly deserved.

In 1940 the 158th Arizona National Guard was called into active duty and attached to the 45th Division. The desert soldiers were sent to Panama and trained in jungle warfare. While training, they dubbed themselves the "Bushmasters" for the deadly snake that inhabited the

Navajo Code Talkers saved thousands of American lives during World War II. They developed a code for transmitting battle plans that kept English-speaking Japanese intelligence officers in a constant state of confusion.

jungles. In 1943 the Arizonans shipped out for the South Pacific and took part in the island-hopping campaigns through the invasion of the Philippines. Tokyo Rose, Japan's propaganda queen, called them the "Butchers of the Pacific." Two months after the bombing of Hiroshima and Nagasaki, they were sent as part of the occupational army to Yokahama, Japan. The 158th finally came home in 1946.

Black soldiers had been stationed at Fort Huachuca since the Apache Wars. The 25th Infantry Regiment, one of the

Lincoln Ragsdale.

original black regiments organized in 1866, was absorbed into the 93rd Division. After they shipped out to the South Pacific, the 92nd Division arrived at Huachuca to train for the European theater. Black troops were also stationed in Williams for a time during the war, guarding military shipments along Route 66.

The 158th Arizona National Guard.

ARIZONA'S WARTIME ECONOMY

☀ *The economy in Arizona changed dramatically during the war. Cotton and copper saw boom times again, as expected, and huge government contracts gave rise to the manufacturing industry. The decade marked the end of agriculture as the chief provider. The Garrett Corporation (later known as Allied Signal) made parts for B-17 bombers. Goodyear Aircraft Corporation had large contracts with the Navy. The company evolved into Goodyear Aerospace Corporation as part of Goodyear Tire and Rubber. Alcoa ran the world's largest aluminum plant, but they later sold to the Reynolds Corporation.*

During the war the state's African-American population grew to about twenty-six thousand residents. Lincoln Ragsdale, a long-time community activist and civic leader, was one of the famous Tuskegee Airmen, black fighter pilots of the 99th Squadron whose skills were proven over Europe during the war. There was a persistent myth in the Air Corps that blacks didn't have the skills to become good fighter pilots. The exemplary record of the Tuskegee Airmen laid that myth to permanent rest.

Wartime Politics

ON THE POLITICAL SCENE, the two-party system was slowly emerging in Arizona. In 1942 and 1944 Democrats registered more than 87 percent of the voters. The only way the Republicans could get anything passed was to form coalitions with the conservative Democrats, who were always fighting with the moderates.

Arizona's wartime governor was Sidney P. Osborn, the only governor to be elected to four consecutive terms. (Before 1974 the term of office for governor was only two years.) He was the scion of a pioneer family. His father had been a page in the first territorial legislature of Prescott in 1864, and his grandfather had been one of the founders of the city of Phoenix. In addition to the war, Osborn had to deal with many other important issues, such as the Colorado River Compact to speed up the plans for using Arizona's 2.8-million-acre-feet allotment suggested by the 1928 Swing-Johnson Bill.

Osborn died in office of Lou Gehrig's Disease (amyotrophic lateral sclerosis) in 1948. He is rated by historians as one of the best governors in the state's history.

Coming Home

IT WAS 1946, the war was over, and America was returning to normalcy once again. Returning GIs wanted three things: girls, sleep, and home cooking. But reality set in soon enough and a fourth item was added to the list: Jobs! They all be-longed to what became known as the "52-20 Club." Ex-GIs got $20 a week for a year while they adjusted to civilian life. Veterans were also going to school on the GI Bill. Married vets got $90 a month, single guys got $72. The GI Bill turned out to be the best investment this country ever made, and it was the result of legislation introduced by Arizona Senator Ernest W. "Mac" McFarland.

With veterans going off to college, enrollment at Arizona State College in Tempe doubled between September 1945 and January 1946 to 1,163 students. At Phoenix College four hundred ex-GIs signed up for classes in one week, doubling the size of the institution.

During the 1940s men's and women's fast-pitch softball games drew large crowds all over the state. Two of the top women's softball teams in the country were the Phoenix A-1 Queens and the PBSW Ramblers. Women's teams drew seven thousand fans to games when the population of Phoenix was only sixty thousand.

The advent of television and air conditioning caused people to "cocoon" in their homes and brought about the demise of the great ball teams of the era. But in 1948 nearly three hundred thousand fans around the U.S. and Canada came out to the ball parks to see the Queens play. During one stretch, the team reached the finals or semifinals twelve out of thirteen times.

The Queens were led by All-American center fielder Dodie Nelson and Skipper Armstrong, while pitcher Margie Law and catcher Dot Wilkinson led the Ramblers. Margie Law was the only player to be named All-American at three positions: pitcher, outfield, and first base. Her husband Kenny was also a champion fast-pitch ball player. He was

PLAYING BALL

✳ *Because of the shortage of men, women's professional baseball teams had been organized during the war. Charlotte "Skipper" Armstrong of Phoenix was one of the women who played in the All-American Girls Professional Baseball League. She signed on as a pro while still in high school. Armstrong is also listed in* Ripley's Believe It Or Not *for pitching both ends of a double-header for the South Bend Blue Sox in 1945. She threw shutouts in both games: One went fifteen innings, the other, seventeen innings. During the late forties and fifties, she pitched for the Phoenix A-1 Queens women's professional softball team, where she was a five-time All-American.*

Skipper Armstrong in her Queens regalia.

THE INCREDIBLE SHRINKING TRANSISTOR

On June 30, 1948, a low-key announcement came from Bell Labs, regarding what is arguably the most important invention of the twentieth century. That day research director Ralph Brown told a group of perplexed reporters, "We have a transistor."

The incredible shrinking transistor would become the basic building block of the modern electronic age. It gave birth to solid-state electronics, the integrated circuit, the personal computer, and the information age.

The transistor is a solid-state electronic device that controls the flow of electrical current, and also acts as a switch, turning current on and off, replacing the bulky, inefficient vacuum tubes of an earlier era. The transistor continues to shrink at a rapid pace as scientists apply theory to practicality, finding new materials that conduct electricity with more precision. Today, millions and soon billions of transistors can fit on a chip a fraction of the size of a vacuum tube.

A year after the invention of the transistor, Motorola opened the first of several electronic plants in Arizona, marking the beginning of the state's high-tech industry. Motorola was followed by IBM, Honeywell, Hughes Aircraft, General Electric, and Sperry. These companies brought a more diversified and balanced economy to the state, and by the 1960s manufacturing became the state's number one income-producing industry. Metropolitan Phoenix is now the nation's third-largest high-tech area.

named most valuable player in the 1948 men's national softball tournament. A year later he struck out seventy-nine batters, a record that still stands, on the way to being named top pitcher in the tourney.

Dot Wilkinson was arguably the best woman athlete in Arizona history. The catcher for the Ramblers was named All-American an amazing nineteen times during her career. She also was a national champion woman bowler.

THE FIRST TEAM to hold spring training was the Detroit Tigers, who trained in Phoenix in 1929. They only stayed a year. In 1947 Bill Veeck brought his Cleveland Indians to train in Tucson. He talked Horace Stoneham into bringing his New York Giants to Phoenix. (During the fifties several more teams moved west, and the Cactus League was born.)

In 1949, the legendary Connie Mack was celebrating his fiftieth year in Major League Baseball as manager of the Philadelphia Athletics. One of his star pitchers that year was Alex Kellner of Tucson. Kellner began his professional career in the early 1940s pitching for the Class C minor league Tucson Cowboys.

The Tucson Cowboys, Arizona-Texas League Champions, 1941.
Alex Kellner is on the far right in the top row.

Breaking Ground

THE YEAR 1948 saw the end of an era that had begun in 1893 as the last electric streetcar made its final run in Phoenix. Around this time, folks traveling to Prescott on the old Black Canyon Highway ran out of pavement south of New River. A narrow, winding road led up to Bumble Bee, thence to Cordes, Mayer, Humboldt, Dewey, and into Prescott. The most popular route was "way out Wickenburg way" and up steep Yarnell Hill, through the mountains to Prescott.

In 1949 beautiful Jacque Mercer, Miss Arizona, would become the first Arizonan to be crowned Miss America.

Also in 1949, nineteen-year-old Emory Sekaquaptewa, a Hopi from Oraibi, become the first full-blooded Native American to receive an appointment to the United States Military Academy at West Point.

CLEANING THE SLATE

☀ *During the war, Phoenix had become a wild and woolly town, with gambling and prostitution rampant. Thousands of soldiers on weekend passes with money in their pockets were easy marks. Someone claimed the town was so tough that at the bowling alleys people bowled overhand. One lonely soldier claimed that he phoned up Dial-A-Prayer, and a voice on the other end told him to "go to hell."*

When the military threatened to declare Phoenix off limits, city fathers decided to clean up the good ol' boy politics that had been running things. A new reform slate was selected, and in 1949 a young reformer named Barry Goldwater launched his career in public service.

The Passing of History

THE FORTIES saw the passing of two outstanding Arizona women. In 1942 the great Hopi potter Nampeyo passed away at the age of eighty-two at her home at Hano on First Mesa. Born in 1860, she was referred to by collectors of Hopi pottery as "the old lady."

Assisting archaeologists with the excavation of Sityatki in 1895, Nampeyo's husband collected potsherds to show his wife. The bold and beautiful designs inspired her to take Hopi pottery to a much higher artistic and technical level. As trading posts began to sell Indian art around the turn of the century, Nampeyo's work fetched top dollar, and was much-sought by collectors. Fred Harvey displayed her work at his famous Harvey Houses and considered her the Southwest's best potter.

Around 1915 her eyesight began failing, and by 1920 she was blind. Although blind, Nampeyo continued to mold and shape her pottery. The designs were painted by her husband, Lesou, until his death in 1935. In typical Hopi custom, Nampeyo shared her talents with other Hopi potters, and she is credited as being responsible for the birth of contemporary Hopi pottery.

On April 8, 1943, Arizona's first state historian, Sharlot Mabridth Hall, died in her hometown of Prescott. Traveling with her emigrant family from Kansas in 1880, eleven-year-old Sharlot rode into Arizona on horseback. She grew up on the Orchard Ranch near Dewey and began her career writing poetry and articles for newspapers and magazines. She became well known around the territory in 1904–05 for her articles attacking the bill for joint statehood with New Mexico.

In 1909 Governor Richard Sloan appointed Hall territorial historian, making her the first woman to hold a territorial post. A spinal injury caused by a fall from a horse limited the spirited woman's work, but in the late twenties she dedicated her life to restoring the old territorial governor's mansion in Prescott. She leased the neglected building, which had fallen into disrepair, and set up residence, collecting materials and raising money to create what has become one of the state's finest museums. Today that museum bears her name.

FUTURE HISTORIANS will likely divide the history of Arizona into two eras, Early and Modern. The Early Period will begin with prehistoric times and conclude with the Great Depression. World War II will be the dividing line. The Modern Period will begin with the postwar years, when high technology industries and tourism replaced mining and agriculture as the state's major economic forces. Affordable air conditioning also came along about this time, making it easier to survive the summer heat. The resulting population growth would exceed even the most optimistic expectations.

1950-1959

THE NIFTY FIFTIES

"I wanted to marry her when I saw the moonlight shining on the barrel of her father's shotgun."

—Eddy Albert in the movie, *Oklahoma!*,
filmed on location in Arizona

"Ah act the way ah feel."

—Elvis Presley, 1955

T HE "NIFTY FIFTIES" SPAWNED BOMB SHELTERS, drive-in movies, Hula Hoops, rock-and-roll, cruising or dragging main street, 3-D movies, car hops, Bob's Big Boy hamburgers, Little League baseball, and Elvis. Haircuts ranged from duck tails to flat tops. Superblonde Marilyn Monroe was the undisputed sex queen and James Dean, with his trademark mumble, was every young girl's heartthrob. Dean defined the teenager fighting conformity. He drove fast, lived hard, and died young, on September 30, 1955, on a narrow highway near Paso Robles, California, when his white Porsche crashed.

In 1956 a former truck driver from Tupelo, Mississippi, named Elvis Presley, hit the big time with a twisting, shimmying, rockabilly sound that opened up a whole new market for six-string guitars. On March 24, 1958, Elvis reported for a two-year tour of duty in the Army. His pay went from excess of $100,000 a month to $83.20. He took it all in good stride saying, "I'm looking forward to serving in the army. I think it will be a great experience for me."

Another musical giant of the fifties was Buddy Holly. His career lasted only eighteen months, yet he wrote and recorded some of the most memorable music to come from the rock-and-roll era. He had nine top-ten hits, including "Peggy Sue" and "That'll Be the Day." On February 3, 1959, Holly and fellow rock-and-roll stars J. P. "Big Bopper" Richardson and Ritchie Valens all died in a plane crash near Mason City, Iowa, and millions of fans went into mourning.

A Superstar from Glendale

ONE OF THE TOP COUNTRY SINGERS of the fifties was Marty Robbins of Glendale. In 1959 Robbins recorded his signature song, "El Paso," and it won a coveted Grammy Award, the first country-and-western song to win such recognition. The song went to number one on both pop and country charts, marking the beginning of bridging the gap between the two music fields.

He got the idea for "El Paso" when driving through the city in 1955, on his way to a family gathering. Two years later, passing through the town again, the song took shape in his mind as he visualized a western melodrama about a young cowboy who fell in love with a Mexican girl in a place in El Paso called Rosa's Cantina—actually Rosa's Cafe in Glendale where he used to hang out. Robbins didn't know it, but there actually was a saloon in El Paso around the turn of the century called Rosa's Cantina.

Glendale's Marty Robbins.

Robbins met his future wife, Marizona, in an ice cream parlor in Glendale. She was also a native Arizonan, her unusual name a contraction of Maricopa and Arizona.

Friendly and approachable, Robbins became one of the Opry's most popular performers. On October 11, 1982, he was inducted in the Country Music Hall of Fame. Two months later, on December 8, he died following open-heart surgery.

Robbins had eighteen number-one hits but is best remembered for the song "El Paso." The folks in that Texas town were so grateful they have a plaque honoring him at the city airport.

Marty Robbins, whose gunfighter ballads became instant cowboy classics.

Rex Allen of Willcox.

Arizona's Singing Cowboys

REX ALLEN, "The Arizona Cowboy" and the last of Hollywood's singing cowboys, was a native of Willcox. He was the only one of the genre who could claim to have been a real cowboy. Blessed with good looks and a mellifluous voice, he was a recording star with several hits when Hollywood called in 1949. He made dozens of movies, had his own television series, and narrated many Walt Disney specials.

Stan Jones was a youngster riding on the D Hill Ranch with an old cowpoke named Cap Watts

**Stan Jones of Douglas,
who wrote the legendary cowboy song,
"Ghost Riders in the Sky."**

when dark, brooding clouds began to build over the Chiricahua Mountains nearby. The old man gazed at the massive, fast-moving clouds that were creating spectral figures. "Ghost riders," he warned prophetically. "We'd better get outta here before they come and take us." Jones never forgot that moment when Cap recounted the old story of

OKLAHOMA IN ARIZONA

☀ *In the mid-fifties Hollywood came out to the historic San Rafael Ranch east of Nogales and filmed Rogers and Hammerstein's,* Oklahoma! *Apparently, the rolling, grass-carpeted hills of southern Arizona more closely resembled the Sooner State. This didn't set well with Oklahomans, who resented the fact that Arizona was chosen for a film about their state. The filmmakers did have a problem growing corn and citrus in the arid land, so they substituted wax for the real thing. Each morning before the cameras started rolling, the production crew carefully hung the wax fruit and vegetables on the plants. There was another problem; the hot Arizona sun kept melting the wax.*

Gordon McRae and Shirley Jones in the "Surrey with the Fringe on Top."

the phantom riders trying to catch the devil's herd. Many years later Jones sat down and wrote the haunting words to the song "Ghost Riders in the Sky."

Jones was working in Death Valley, California, as a park ranger in 1949 when his life changed overnight. Acting as a guide for movie location scouts on the film *Three Godfathers* (starring John Wayne, Harry Carry, Jr., and Pedro Armendariz), he sang the haunting lyrics about the ghost riders one night around a campfire. A year later he was appearing in the movie *Riders In The Sky* with Gene Autry.

Later Jones wrote other hit songs, including the theme song from the John Wayne classic *The Searchers,* and the hit song, *Cowpoke,* recorded by many singers, including Eddy Arnold and Arizona resident Glen Campbell.

PRICE INDEX

✺ *A pair of Justin cowboy boots were still selling for the same price as a decade ago, $36.50. A Stetson cowboy hat had gone up to $22.50, and a pair of Levi's now cost $4.19. In Arizona, gas sold for 27 cents a gallon, a new car cost less than $1,500, and $9,000 could put you in a new home. In 1954 bread was 17 cents a loaf and coffee was 65 cents a pound.*

A Front-Row Seat for Baseball's Golden Age

IN THE SPRING OF 1951 the World Champion New York Yankees came to Phoenix to train at the old Phoenix Municipal stadium on Central and Mohave streets. One of the team's owners, Del Webb, was from Phoenix and he wanted to show the team off to locals. He worked a trade with the Giants to swap training camps for a year.

This was years before professional basketball, football, and hockey became popular spectator sports. New York's baseball teams—the Yankees,

Dodgers, and Giants—battled it out year after year for sports supremacy. The mighty Yankees had been in the World Series so many times even their bench warmers were household names.

That spring Arizonans got to watch the grand finale of one superstar and the birth of another. It would be Joe DiMaggio's last year in baseball. His replacement was nineteen-year-old Mickey Mantle, a muscular youngster with a boyish grin and all-American looks from Commerce, Oklahoma. It was also the rookie season for another kid who would become one of the game's greatest players, Willie Mays. Early in the season the Giants brought up Willie Mays from the minors, overcoming a Dodger lead of thirteen games to win what became known as the "Miracle of Coogan's Bluff."

✳ *By 1950 Phoenix was at a disadvantage in its search for new industry because of the sparseness of its cultural life. Maie Bartlett Heard donated land at Central and McDowell for a new civic complex that included a library, the Phoenix Little Theater, and an art museum, which became the world-famous Phoenix Art Museum and opened in 1959. Not included was a civic auditorium—that dream would have to wait another decade to be realized.*

Modern Science

BETWEEN 1955 AND 1958, astronomers looked at more than 150 mountain peaks in the Southwest before choosing Kitt Peak, near Tucson, as the site of a new astronomical observatory. There are twenty-two telescopes of all shapes and sizes clustered on the peak, which reaches an elevation of 6,900 feet. The Kitt Peak Observatory is today funded by the

National Science Foundation and managed by two dozen universities. Fore-most is the University of Arizona in Tucson.

Barrow Neurological Institute, located in St. Joseph's Hospital and Medical Center, was endowed in 1958 by industrialist Charles Barrow of Phoenix. Barrow pledged to donate $500,000 to the hospital if matching funds could be obtained. His wife died of a brain tumor at St. Joseph's, and over the years he became very close to the hospital. He eventually donated close to two million dollars to the Institute, which opened in 1962. Three years later, the first fund raiser, the annual Barrow Ball, was held. In later decades, several ground-breaking medical procedures would be pioneered at Barrow Neurological Institute.

Close to the Brink

IN 1950 Arizona had a population of 750,000 residents. The city of Phoenix covered only seventeen square miles and had a population of 107,000. By the end of the decade the state had grown to 1.3 million and the capital city had nearly 450,000 residents. By then manufacturing had become the number one income-producing industry.

In 1950 Communism was out to conquer the world. Josef Stalin's Russia had three times the combat airplanes as the United States, thirty tank divisions to our one, and four times as many soldiers under arms. But the United States had an ace card . . . we were the only ones with an atomic bomb. We were, that is, until late summer 1949 when Russia exploded Joe One (for Josef Stalin).

In schools across Arizona children were trained to get under their desks to avoid being injured by an atomic bomb. This writer was raised in the small town of Ash Fork, in the northern part of the state. Local residents were inspired to wonder aloud, "why would the Russians want to waste an atomic bomb on Ash Fork?"

The two countries moved closer to the brink on June 25, 1950, when Communist soldiers from North Korea swarmed across the 38th Parallel and rolled into South Korea. A small, ill-equipped force of American soldiers were sent to hold the line, but in a matter of weeks American and

South Korean troops were pushed into a small area in the southeast part of the peninsula that became known as the Pusan Beachhead.

Then, in a bold stroke of military genius, General Douglas MacArthur sent the First Marine Division ashore at Inchon, far behind the North Korean lines. The North Korean army was virtually destroyed, and soon the Americans were sweeping deep into North Korea. In November Chinese "volunteers" entered the war, sending hundreds of divisions across the Yalu River and overwhelming the Americans. In one of the most dramatic retreats in American history, U.S. soldiers and Marines began a pullout towards the Chosin Reservoir. Despite the defeat, it was a proud moment in military history as the soldiers fought their way to ships waiting at the port city of Hungnam. The American soldiers inflicted heavy casualties upon the Chinese, but the Reds had a seemingly inexhaustible number of bodies to throw at them. Legendary Marine General Lewis B. "Chesty" Puller was heard to remark, "The Chinese are on our right, the North Koreans are on our left, both are coming at us head on, and the ocean's at our backs. By God, they won't get away from us this time."

Ash Fork in 1953.

Eventually the battle lines stabilized near the original dividing line between North and South Korea and remained in that area until a truce was finally declared on July 27, 1953. However, the war has never been officially declared over. A total of 36,914 Americans died in this so-called "forgotten war." Among them were 171 Arizonans.

Peace talks with the Chinese and North Koreans began in July 1951 and dragged on tirelessly. *Arizona Republic* political cartoonist Reg Manning won a Pulitzer Prize in 1951 with a drawing of silk top hats worn by diplomats hanging on a hat rack. The other half of the rendering showed a GI's helmet hanging on a small, wooden cross.

The Arizona Political Scene

IN 1950, for the first time in Arizona history, a woman was a major-party candidate for governor. Ana Frohmiller, twelve times elected state auditor, was referred to in a national magazine as the "watchdog of the Arizona treasury." She'd emerged the winner from a large field of Democratic candidates. Her opponent was J. Howard Pyle, who'd won fame for his interviews with Arizona soldiers during World War II. His campaign manager was novice politician Barry Goldwater.

Ana Frohmiller.

At the time, Democrats held a voter registration advantage of nine to two. Many Arizonans weren't ready to vote for a woman, and there was some talk of members of the Ku Klux Klan appearing at one of Frohmiller's rallies. During a speech in Globe, a member of the media asked Frohmiller what her thoughts were on the Klan. With a straight face she replied, "I don't trust any man under the sheets."

Despite the overwhelming Democratic margin, Republican Howard Pyle won the gubernatorial election. Still, the

Democrats won all nineteen Senate seats and sixty-one of seventy-two House seats.

Howard Pyle had been a reluctant candidate. Barry Goldwater had talked him into running in the uphill battle for the governor's office, so in 1952 Pyle returned the favor. He persuaded Goldwater to run against Senate Majority Leader Ernest W. McFarland. Considering the overwhelming Democratic majority in voter registration, it seemed an impossible task. However, the immensely popular Dwight D. Eisenhower was the 1952 Republican Party candidate for president, and that would make a difference. Goldwater, a pilot, flew all over the state, running a grassroots campaign. Meanwhile, Washington business kept McFarland busy and he was never able to sustain a strong campaign. When the results were in, Goldwater had pulled off the most stunning political upset in the state's history.

Ernest W. McFarland, a former Pinal County judge and the father of the GI Bill, had himself pulled an upset victory in the primaries of 1940, unseating Senator Henry Fountain Ashurst. He would later serve two terms as governor and become Chief Justice of the State Supreme Court, the only person in the nation to hold top positions in all three branches of state government.

The 1952 political conventions were televised, and the public got its first ringside seat to the slugfest to see who would be the party nominees. They turned out to be the eloquent, witty Illinois governor, Adlai Stevenson, and popular World War II General Dwight "Ike" Eisenhower.

The Short Creek Raid

IN THE 1950s, the issue of religious freedom surfaced in an unusual way. Polygamy had been outlawed in the Mormon church in the 1890s, but some fundamentalist groups continued the practice. In the early predawn hours of July 26, 1953, eighty-nine officers of the Arizona Highway Patrol closed in on the little town of Short Creek, a polygamist community. Short Creek was located on the remote Arizona Strip along the border with Utah. The residents of the tiny community, many of them combat veterans, knew the raid was coming. Instead of resisting, they gathered peacefully at the plaza and awaited the arrival of the state troopers. One hundred residents were served warrants, charging them with such crimes as statutory rape, polygamy, bigamy, and adultery. The men were gathered up and hauled off in buses to jail at Kingman. Short Creek was on the north side of the Grand Canyon, so in order to get to the county seat it was necessary to drive into Utah, then across to Nevada, and back into Arizona.

The women and children of the polygamist families were taken on buses to Phoenix, where they were placed in foster homes and social services centers. It was like a time warp. Their clothing was similar to that worn in the 1880s. The children were enrolled in Phoenix schools, attending classes looking like reenactors in some drama of pioneer days. It was an unfortunate situation, and although Governor Pyle believed he was doing the right thing by raiding Short Creek, many Arizonans were offended by the manner in which the raid was conducted and the aftermath. Pyle was defeated in the next election. Afterward, locals changed the name of the community to Colorado City.

Today, there is a plaque commemorating the event in the plaza in Colorado City. The citizens of the community regard their experience as a test of their faith and remain proud for standing up for their beliefs.

The Cycle of Bust and Boom

IN 1959 Phoenix was experiencing boom times. More construction was done in Phoenix in that year than in all the years from 1914 to 1946 combined. That same year Arizona State College at Tempe became Arizona State University.

Meanwhile, as shopping malls like Park Central, Christown, and Thomas Mall were established on the outer fringes of Phoenix, downtown shopping went into decline. Downtown stores such as Goldwater's, Diamonds, Hanny's, and Korrick's opened anchor stores in the new malls.

Tourism became a major industry in Arizona following the Second

World War as Americans and foreigners had more discretionary money to travel. Historically, the northern part of the state had been isolated from the rest of it by rugged mountains, but by the end of the decade the old Black Canyon highway was paved all the way from Phoenix to Prescott. The days of driving on a dirt road to Payson ended in 1959 when Highway 87, the Beeline Highway, was completed.

Communities with great climates such as Bisbee, Prescott, and Flagstaff, which found themselves bypassed by free-

Stylish woman of the 1950s.

ways or victims of closing copper mines, had to create other opportunities for economic growth. Blessed with uniquely designed architectural structures from bygone days, these communities restored and reopened their historic buildings as restaurants, bars, and shops.

Phelps Dodge closed down the mines at the "Billion Dollar Copper Camp" of Jerome in 1953, and the town that once boasted a population of fifteen thousand began to reinvent itself as a ghost town. Jerome High School consolidated with Clarkdale and became Mingus High School. Most of the homes and stores were boarded up and fell into disrepair. But during the 1960s artists began moving into the hillside community, creating a revival as a trendy art colony that continues to this day.

THE PHOENIX GIANT

By the time the fifties came to a close Phoenix had a Triple-A baseball franchise as a farm team for the San Francisco Giants. The city built a new baseball park in Papago Park for the team. Fans could go out and watch future major league players like Willie McCovey do their thing. Former Yankee pitcher Don Larsen, who pitched the only perfect game in World Series history—against the Dodgers in 1956—hurled for the Phoenix Giants in the late fifties on the downside of his career.

The Arizona-Texas League

IN THE EARLY 1950S, long before big-league professional sports came to Arizona and when baseball was still just a game, the newspaper sports pages devoted front-page coverage to the Arizona-Texas League, Class-C minor league baseball. Phoenix, Tucson, Bisbee-Douglas, and Globe-Miami made up the state's contingent in the league. One of those who made it all the way to the big show was Billy Martin. He played (and battled) the 1947 season for the Phoenix Senators in the old stadium on south Central Avenue and Mohave.

In 1953 Arizona sports writers and fans focused their attention on a pitcher for the Tucson Cowboys named Corkey Reddell. Reddell was a native of Scottsdale and grew up on a farm where the Civic Plaza is today. Scottsdale was a town of only about two thousand people in those days, so small they had to put a mirror next to it so it'd seem larger. They had to share their one horse with another town. Motel 6 built there and called it Motel 3. There were no traffic lights, but lots of stop signs, causing outsiders to dub the place Stopsdale.

Old-timers tell a story (this writer won't vouch for the veracity) about a scout who'd heard of Reddell and came to check him out. He found Reddell in Indian Bend Wash knocking down jackrabbits with stones. He'd spot one forty yards away, rear back, and make a perfect left-handed throw, hitting the critter upside the head every time. The scout was confused. His reports all said Reddell was a right-hander, but he was throwing rocks at better than ninety-five m.p.h. with his left. After introducing himself, the scout said, "Son, I've been told you're a right-hander."

"I am," Reddell replied.

"Then why are you throwing at those jackrabbits with your left?"

Reddell grinned and said, "Because when I use my right arm it ruins the meat."

There were a number of other baseball yarns spun about Corkey Reddell but the above is the only one that has any credibility; the others are tall tales.

Left-hander Corkey Reddell.

Reddell became the ace hurler for the Tucson Cowboys. In one magical season, 1953, he had a year most pitchers would kill for, no matter what level. That year Arizonans watched in awe as he chalked up victory after victory for the Cowboys. It seemed like he was pitching every other game. When the season ended he'd won an amazing twenty-eight games while losing only five. Earlier, New York Giants manager Leo Durocher refused to give Reddell a tryout, saying he was too small to be a ball player. Later that year Durocher presented the Arizona Athlete of the Year award, and the man receiving the award was Corkey Reddell.

Many old Arizona-Texas League baseball fans remember Reddell's amazing 1953 season. Few, however, recall that he was a pretty good hitter, too. During the 1954 season he hit .669 as a pitcher. He was fourteen for twenty-four, with one home run and four doubles. Not bad for a country boy from Scottsdale.

Unfortunately, Corkey Reddell's career in baseball was brief. Pitching all those games that season took a toll on his pitching arm, and he never was the same. He pitched for and managed the Globe-Miami Browns for a year before returning to Scottsdale.

This writer was a seventeen-year-old catcher playing for the semipro Glendale Greys in 1956, when I came to bat against Cork. By then he was back pitching for the Scottsdale Blues in Arizona's semiprofessional league. His tired pitching arm was only a shadow of what it had been three years earlier, but I still couldn't hit him.

Years later I became friends with Charlie Grimm, the great scout for the Chicago Cubs. He told me a good story about Corkey Reddell. He said a fan from Tucson approached him about signing the pitcher. "I saw Reddell pitch fourteen innings in Juarez and strike out every batter," the fan gushed. "Only one guy touched the ball and that was a weak, opposite-field foul ball."

Charlie's eyes brightened. "What was the name of the guy who hit the foul ball?"

"I dunno, why?" the fan asked.

"The Cubs need hitters," Charlie said.

NEW FRONTIERS

"We stand on the edge of a New Frontier."

—John Fitzgerald Kennedy, July 1960

"Extremism in the defense of liberty is no vice."

—Barry Goldwater, acceptance speech
for the Republican party presidential nomination, July 1964

T HE POSTWAR YEARS OF THE FORTIES had been full of hope. In the fifties we were bystanders and observers. In the sixties we participated. The sixties have been called the decade of revolution. In reality, much of what is perceived to belong to the sixties happened in the decade that followed. The sixties began as a rather quiet extension of the fifties. Television shows like *Father Knows Best, Leave It to Beaver, The Andy Griffith Show,* and *My Three Sons* portrayed families as stable institutions. The Kingston Trio was the top folk music group in the country. Their songs, reflecting the times, were mostly lighthearted and fun. Light comedy films like *Pillow Talk,* starring Rock Hudson and Doris Day, were big hits at the box office.

John Fitzgerald Kennedy defeated Richard Nixon for president in a close race. America became enamored with Camelot. But beneath the veneer of tranquillity, trouble was brewing. The Bay of Pigs invasion in Cuba was a fiasco, and the Cuban missile crisis brought America and Russia to the brink. Then America began to get entangled into the morass that was Vietnam. By 1964 the situation was escalating into a full-scale war.

Everybody who was alive then remembers exactly what they were doing on November 22, 1963, when President John F. Kennedy was assassinated in Dallas. Vice President Lyndon Baines Johnson became president.

Baby boomers were now young adults: Half of America was under twenty-five and Bob Dylan was the minstrel for the new times. He wrote, "The Times They Are A-Changin'," and they were. The social and political fabric was splitting at the seams. By the mid-1960s all hell broke loose. Normalcy was out; rebellion was in. Young people were committed to change, and change we did. Word processors of the sixties were mimeograph machines and these young rebels pasted America with flyers and leaflets.

They preached love, peace, and euphoria, and if they couldn't find it naturally, they did it with doses of grass, LSD, and mescaline. Signs of the times included long hair, Afros, the Pill, Janis Joplin, Haight-Ashbury, flower children, freedom riders, and the sexual revolution. Young women ceremoniously burned their bras. Young men burned their draft cards and exiled themselves to Canada and Mexico. Those who remained placed daisies in the rifle barrels of soldiers guarding the Pentagon.

Arizona Politics

MEANWHILE, IN WASHINGTON,, Barry Goldwater wasn't the only Arizonan making a name for himself. In 1961 Representative Stewart L. Udall, scion of a pioneer Mormon family, became Secretary of the Interior in the new Kennedy Administration. He was the first Arizonan to be appointed to a cabinet post. Udall's younger brother Morris, "Mo," replaced him in Congress. Mo Udall went on to become one of

Arizonans who played prominent roles in national politics. Left to right: John Rhodes (entered Congress in 1953 and rose to House Minority Leader before retiring in 1983), Barry Goldwater, Paul Fannin (was governor from 1959 to 1965 and served in the U.S. Senate from 1965 to 1977), Morris Udall, and Carl Hayden (an Arizona legend, entered Congress with statehood in 1912 and went to the U.S. Senate in 1927 where he served until retiring in 1969).

the most popular and respected politicians in Washington. He had a Lincolnesque sense of humor that endeared him to Democrats and Republicans alike.

Since statehood in 1912, Arizona's small rural counties were able to retain political control over the large urban counties. Agriculture and mining interests controlled most of the state's politics. For example, in 1954 the Senate was reapportioned to twenty-eight members, two from each county. Although Pima and Maricopa counties had over seventy percent of the population, the top three Senate leadership positions were controlled by the rural counties.

All this changed in 1966 when a federal court reapportioned the legislature on a basis of "one-man, one-vote." Across the nation, state legislatures were required to reapportion districts to represent an equal number of people. In Arizona the ruling apportioned fifteen senators and twelve representatives to Maricopa County. A year after reapportionment, the Republicans gained control of the legislature for the first time. Today the state is divided into thirty districts with thirty senators and sixty representatives.

Transportation Milestones

THE YEAR 1960 marked two milestones in Arizona transportation history. The first freeway segment, the Black Canyon freeway (I-17 near Grand Avenue), was completed. The Maricopa freeway segment proceeded east from that first section. Also that year, a grid of freeways was mapped throughout the Valley, including the Papago, Squaw Peak, Outer Loop, and Paradise. Forty years later the results are beginning to come to fruition. During the sixties freeways were believed to be the wave of the future, but in the early seventies *The Arizona Republic* reversed itself and came out against freeways. Thanks to a barrage of antifreeway editorials, the Papago Freeway was voted down in 1973, setting freeway construction back ten to fifteen years, according to Valley historians.

The Black Canyon freeway, or Interstate-17, began construction north along old State Highway 69 in 1954. (During the forties the old Black Canyon highway passed through Bumble Bee, Cordes, Mayer, Humboldt, and Dewey. Later, Highway 69 branched off Interstate-17 at Cordes Junction.) Up to the 1960s the most sensible way to travel from Phoenix to Flagstaff was to go by way of Prescott and Ash Fork, a journey of 220 miles. The paving of the more direct Interstate-17 in the late sixties cut nearly a hundred miles off the trip, effectively linking northern and central Arizona. It was completed in 1973. Other interstates completed during that time included I-10 from Phoenix to Tucson in 1965, and I-8 from Casa Grande to Yuma in 1971.

Lorna Lockwood

DURING THE 1960s Lorna Lockwood became the first woman in America to be named chief justice of a state Supreme Court. The Arizona Women's Hall of Fame used ten words to capsulize Judge Lorna Lockwood's career: Lawyer, legislator, Superior Court judge, state Supreme Court chief justice.

Lockwood was born in Douglas in 1903 and graduated from high school at Tombstone. She attended law school at the University of Arizona, where one of her classmates was Nellie Bush, airplane pilot and riverboat skipper on the

Lorna Lockwood was the first woman to sit as Chief Justice of a state supreme court.

Colorado River. Bush later served in the Arizona Senate. Once when they were in law school, the subject of rape was on the agenda, and the dean of the school decreed that no women students would be allowed to participate. Bush and Lockwood went to the dean and demanded to know if he could recall a case of rape where a woman hadn't participated. He had no answer to their logic, so he relented. The women attended the seminar in triumph.

Lockwood's father was a lawyer and judge. He served on the state Supreme Court from 1925 to 1942, and was chief justice three times. At an early age she decided to follow in his footsteps. She did: In 1960 she became a justice on the state Supreme Court and chose to occupy her father's desk.

Good-bye, Glen Canyon; Hello, Lake Powell

THE TOWN OF PAGE on the Arizona-Utah border was a planned community from the start, designed by the Bureau of Reclamation to provide headquarters and house workers for the building of Glen Canyon Dam, which was completed in 1963. The town was destined for growth and success as the gateway to the beautiful canyon country and the vast recreational area of Lake Powell. The lake has more than two thousand miles of picturesquely rugged shoreline and extends nearly two hundred miles into Utah. The town was named for John C. Page, who spent years planning and developing the proposed dam site while serving as Commissioner of Reclamation. He died in 1955, never seeing the fruits of his dream.

Nearby is the *Vados de los Padres,* where in 1776 the Franciscan priests Dominguez and Escalante crossed the Colorado River during their unsuccessful attempts to locate a route between Santa Fe and Los Angeles. Prehistoric Indians had once hunted and lived in the side canyons, and during the 1860s prospectors scoured the gulches for gold. Before it was covered with the waters of Lake Powell, Glen Canyon was one of America's most beautiful and primitive wilderness areas.

Glen Canyon was named by Major John Wesley Powell, the one-armed explorer whose history-making expeditions through the Grand Canyon in 1869 and the early 1870s brought fame and recognition to the area. He was awestruck by the beautiful red rock chasm, noting the "carved walls, royal arches, glens, alcove gulches, mounts, and monuments; from which of these features shall we select a name: We decide to call it Glen Canyon."

Arizona's Community Colleges

ARIZONA HAS SOME OF THE BEST community colleges in the nation. The first, Phoenix College, opened its doors in 1920 with fifteen students. By 1962, when the Maricopa County Community College District was created, district enrollment was ten thousand students. Soon new community colleges opened at Mesa and Glendale. In 1969 a new college in Scottsdale opened for classes. (By the 1990s the district was the nation's second largest with more than two hundred thousand students attending classes at ten colleges.)

Honored Arizonans

IN 1966 Governor Sam Goddard named Arizona folksinger Dolan Ellis the state's official balladeer. Ellis was an original member of the New Christy Minstrels, one of the nation's top recording groups. He left the group in the mid-sixties to return to Arizona. Since then he's written and recorded dozens of songs about the state. (In the 1990s he would develop an Arizona Folklore Preserve at Ramsey Canyon in the Huachuca Mountains.)

Anne Dodge Wauneka was presented by President John F. Kennedy with the Medal of Freedom, the nation's highest civilian award, for her work to halt the spread of tuberculosis among Navajos. She was the daughter of Henry Chee Dodge, the last chief of the tribe and first tribal chairman. She was also the first woman to serve on the Navajo Tribal Council. In health care among her people, Wauneka was a leading advocate for hospital treatment in combination with traditional healing. She was also active in promoting social and educational programs in Navajoland.

Another Scottsdale Pitcher

Scottsdale's contribution to professional baseball in the sixties was Jim Palmer. A natural athlete, Palmer was an all-state baseball, basketball, and football player at Scottsdale High School. He signed a professional baseball contract with the Baltimore Orioles. Three years later he was pitching in the 1966 World Series against the great Sandy Koufax and the Los Angeles Dodgers. Before the game the twenty-two-year-old youngster said, "I'll probably have to pitch a shutout to beat Kolfax." That day he blanked the Dodgers 6-0, making him the youngest pitcher ever to throw a shutout in a World Series game.

Jim Palmer in action.

Palmer, a three-time winner of the coveted Cy Young Award, was also the only pitcher to win World Series games in three decades, with wins in 1966, 1970, 1971, and 1983. In nineteen seasons with the Orioles, Palmer had eight twenty-game seasons. In 1990 he became the first homegrown Arizonan to be inducted into the Baseball Hall of Fame at Cooperstown, New York.

In a Tavern in Sedona . . .

In 1965 the world-famous group of painters who call themselves Cowboy Artists of America was born in uptown Sedona at the Oak Creek Tavern. The original founders were cowboy artists Charlie Dye, John Hampton, George Phippen, and Joe Beeler. They created a charter dedicated to "perpetuate the memory and culture of the Old West . . . to insure authentic representation of the life of the West as it was and is."

Prior to the 1960s cowboy artists worked as illustrators for pulp magazines or drew for cowboy comic books. They usually sold their works out of the back of their pickup trucks and the only buyers were ranchers. There wasn't much money to be made in cowboy art. Joe Beeler, a transplanted Oklahoman who decided he could just as well "starve in Sedona as in Oklahoma," moved to Arizona. As Americans had more discretionary money and Texas oil men became flush, cowboy art became a hot item. For Beeler, Phippen, Hampton, and Dye, the timing was perfect.

"We wanted to maintain the integrity of artists like Charlie Russell,"

MIRANDA V. ARIZONA

☀ *In 1963 a truck driver named Ernesto Miranda forced an eighteen-year-old girl into a car, took her out into the desert, and raped her. He was caught, confessed, tried, convicted, and sentenced to twenty to thirty years in prison for kidnapping and rape.*

Two Phoenix attorneys, John Frank and John Flynn, appealed his conviction all the way to the Supreme Court, arguing that police should have advised Miranda of his right to remain silent and his right to consult with a lawyer. On June 13, 1966, the court agreed. The so-called "Miranda rights" ruling requires officers to read suspects their rights and warn them anything they say could be held against them in a court of law.

Miranda's common-law wife testified against him in a second trial, and he went to prison, where he stayed until paroled in 1973. But Miranda hadn't learned his lesson. Three years later, on January 31, 1976, he was stabbed to death in a barroom fight.

Beeler said, and they have succeeded. Members have since shown their works all over the world, making cowboy art popular and lucrative. Today these artists are earning what Russell used to call "dead man's wages" for their work.

Cowboy art, like cowboys themselves, is plainspoken and straightforward. "The difference between modern art and cowboy art," Beeler explained, "is with cowboy art, you don't have to have somebody stand there and tell 'em what it is."

The Fourth of July, 1966

THE VIETNAM WAR touched everyone, but none more than the citizens of the small mining town of Morenci. The year 1966 continues to invoke sad and poignant memories. On July 4, nine recent graduates of Morenci High School, all members of the football team, joined the U.S. Marine Corps. All were in the prime of youth, the cream of the crop at Morenci High. Together, they all went off to boot camp at San Diego, and together, they all came home on leave. The youngsters walked proudly around the old hometown in their Marine uniforms. Drivers honked their horns in recognition as the whole town celebrated the young men's rite of passage. All were sent to Vietnam. Their story has become a local legend.

Of the nine young men who enlisted that Fourth of July, six died in battle. Bobby Dale Proper was an all-state linebacker for the Morenci Wildcats. Stan King was six feet, four inches tall and a three-sport letterman. They, along with Al Van Whitman, Larry West, Jose "Cowboy" Mangayo, and Clive Garcia, gave their lives. *Time* magazine did a story on the youngsters and the town. No community or high school during the war had given so much. The three survivors, Joe Sorrelmon, Mike Cranford, and LeRoy Cisneros, saw extensive combat in the war; the latter was point man on forty-two patrols. They returned home to Morenci and tried to put the war behind them. The old ball field where they played, the high school they attended, even the old town of Morenci is gone, swallowed up by the open-pit mine, and new town was built on a nearby hill. But the memories of those youngsters linger. The story of those six young men who died in the flower of youth is forever woven into the fabric of the history of Morenci.

Barry Goldwater, Renaissance Man

WHEN ARIZONA POLITICAL AFICIONADOS recall the sixties they think of Barry Goldwater, the man who launched modern Conservatism, paving the way for the Reagan presidency in 1980. Goldwater's 1960 book, *Conscience of a Conservative,* won him acclaim and was a major reason for his becoming the Republican party nominee for president.

As a young man, dashing and extremely handsome, Goldwater thrived socially. He was a natural leader but fell down in his studies. Elected class president at Phoenix Union High School, he flunked most of his classes, causing his father to send him to Staunton Military Academy in Virginia. Again, he barely scraped by in scholastics but excelled in sports and leadership. He also acquired a love for the military and wanted to go on to West Point, but his father was ill, so he returned to Phoenix and took a job clerking in the family store for twenty dollars a week.

He attended the University of Arizona for a year before returning to take over the family business, Goldwater's Department Store, upon his father's death. Always generous, he'd read in the morning paper about some family tragedy and direct someone from the store to send clothes anonymously.

Among Goldwater's many

Barry Goldwater at the Prescott Frontier Days parade in 1964.

Former President Dwight D. Eisenhower and
Barry M. Goldwater, ca. 1964.

talents was a genius for marketing. In 1938 he promoted a product that drew national attention, called Antsy Pants. "You'll rant and dance with ants in your pants," the ads claimed. Antsy Pants were white cotton men's undershorts decorated with large red ants. Goldwater said, "I just figured there wasn't a woman in the world that didn't know a man she'd like to send a pair of Antsy Pants." The store was overwhelmed with orders. "We almost went broke selling Antsy Pants," he said later.

He also promoted a "Men's Night." During the Christmas season the store would stay open after hours, serve drinks, and entertain male shoppers with pretty women modeling lingerie. In this he was a man ahead of his time.

During the Christmas season of 1930 he met a young woman named Peggy Johnson who was doing her shopping at Goldwater's. Four years later, he married her in her hometown of Muncie, Indiana. They raised four children and were married fifty-one years before her death in 1985.

With his trademark dark, horn-rimmed glasses, and frank, candid style, Goldwater was a well known icon. He was sometimes cranky, profane, and self-deprecating and was best known for his gruff wit and firm convictions. He was a maverick with the rugged individualism that has characterized westerners throughout history. Politically, Goldwater was always an inpendent thinker. One example of this was his controversial stand against civil rights in 1964. It was his belief that government should stay out of social issues, the classic nineteenth-century libertarian view.

In 1937, at the age of twenty-eight, he became one of the youngest chief executives in America. When war came in 1941, he parleyed his army reserve commission and flying experience into a regular Army Air Corps commission. During the war he served in the China-Burma theater and later ferried planes to England prior to the invasion of Europe.

In 1945 he returned home and organized the Arizona Air National Guard. He eventually retired as a Major General in the Air Force Reserve. In 1949 Goldwater was chosen Phoenix Man of the Year. That same year he was elected to the city council.

The highlight of Goldwater's illustrious political career came on July 16, 1964, at the Cow Palace in San Francisco. That evening he accepted the nomination for the presidency of the United States.

Goldwater was good friends with John F. Kennedy. They'd served in the Senate together during the fifties, and both looked forward to running against each other in the election of 1964. Although at opposite ends of the political spectrum, they had great respect for one another and planned a whistle-stop campaign together for the 1964 presidential race, something that would give voters a clear choice. It was all blowing in the wind after November 22, 1963, when Kennedy was killed and succeeded by Lyndon Baines Johnson. Goldwater knew the nation wouldn't change presidents again in such a short time. He ran in 1964 for the good of the party.

The liberal Eastern wing of the Republican party abandoned Goldwater during the presidential race. Democrats painted him as a reckless right-winger who would order military actions that could involve America in a war. Democrat Lyndon Johnson allowed Goldwater to be portrayed as a hawk and himself as the only hope for peace. Yet, at the same time Johnson was saying, "I will never send American boys to Vietnam," the Johnson administration was secretly running military operations there.

In November, Goldwater lost a lopsided election to Johnson. And the rest, as they say, is history. Goldwater's campaign slogan, "In your heart you know he's right," turned out to be quite prophetic. He lost the battle but won the war. As time went by, Goldwater became more respected than the man who defeated him for the presidency.

He served in the U.S. Senate for thirty years, from 1952 to 1964 and 1968 to 1986, and won the Presidential Medal of Freedom for his service to the nation. He was a statesman known fondly around the world. He ran for president himself and helped convince another president to resign.

Goldwater was very important in Republican party history as he tipped the scales from Eastern domination, increasing the party's power in the West and South. He was the blunt-spoken common man who might be called the Republican Harry Truman. He officially retired from politics in 1986, and unlike many who hang around Washington, he returned to his beloved Arizona.

Had Barry Goldwater never gone into public service he'd have likely become a world-famous photographer. He created the first color cover for the December 1946 issue of *Arizona Highways* magazine. Some two hundred of his photos appeared in the magazine. He filmed a river trip down the Colorado in 1940 lasting some forty-four days. His photos and film of running the Colorado became traveling lectures, giving him great exposure in the state and helping to launch his political career. His greatest honor as a photographer was his election to membership in the Royal Photographic Society of London.

Goldwater had a great respect for Native Americans, evident in his photography. He photographed them with sensitivity, dignity, and realism. At one time, he owned a trading post at Navajo Mountain on the Arizona-Utah border. During fierce winter storms, when the muddy roads were impassable, he airlifted food and supplies. One time Goldwater crash-landed his plane, scattering glass all over the area. Some Navajo medicine men who were apprehensive about people flying carried the shards of broken glass around for years as proof that man was not supposed to fly.

Goldwater had a keen sense of humor, too. During the Navajo-Hopi dispute in the 1970s he sided with the latter, a stance that greatly offended some of his old Navajo friends. This was about the same time they were installing those newfangled voting machines on the reservation. Goldwater was there campaigning, and knowing voters were angry, he offered to assist in teaching them how to use the voting machines. "Take that little needle," he explained, pointing to the little box by his name on the sample ballot, "and stick it in old Barry Goldwater." He won the election.

The Space Race

THE RACE FOR THE MOON began with the decade. The Soviets took the lead with the launching of Sputnik in 1957, and on April 12, 1961, Russia shocked the free world again by sending a man into space.

But America, a nation of explorers and dreamers, wasn't about to cede the space race to the Russians. On May 25, 1961, President Kennedy resolved to restore national prestige when he addressed Congress: "I believe this nation should commit itself to achieving the goal, before this decade is out, of landing a man on the moon and returning him safely to earth." Congress responded by approving the first of $22 billion, 3 percent of the annual federal budget, that would eventually go into Project Apollo.

Two years earlier a new breed of hero had emerged on the American scene: the astronaut. The original seven, Alan Shepard, John Glenn, Donald "Deke" Slayton, Scott Carpenter, Gordon Cooper, Virgil "Gus" Grissom, and Wally Schirra, would pave the way for the exploration of outer space. The first Americans to reach for the stars, they were revered by the American public much like the frontiersmen who explored the West in the nineteenth century. John Stewart of the Kingston Trio penned a fitting song, "New Frontier," with lyrics making that comparison.

On May 5, 1961, Alan Shepard climbed into the tiny Mercury capsule atop a Redstone rocket and blasted off on a fifteen-minute, 302-mile suborbital flight down the Atlantic, paving the way for the assault on the moon eight years later.

Arizona's contribution to the corps of astronauts was Frank Borman of Tucson. As a youngster, Borman quarterbacked the undefeated Tucson High School Badgers to the 1945 Arizona state football championship. He also developed a love of flying.

Neil Armstrong puzzling over a rock formation at the Grand Canyon, 1964.

After high school he attended West Point and graduated with the class of 1950. He qualified for the Air Corps—the Air Force Academy wasn't established until the mid-fifties. He became a fighter pilot and later a test pilot before joining the second generation of astronauts. He flew two of NASA's most dangerous missions.

In December 1965, Borman and Jim Lovell, Jr. spent two weeks in orbit in Gemini 7, in a compartment not much bigger than the front seat of a Volkswagen. They executed the first manned space rendezvous in orbit, linking up with Gemini 6. On December 21, 1968, Borman piloted Apollo 8 into the first moon orbit. His crew was Lovell and Bill Anders. The three men were the first to see the earth in its totality.

Then, on July 24 of the next year, while some six hundred million people around the world sat glued to their television sets, thirty-eight-year-old Neil Armstrong stepped down on the face of the moon and proclaimed, "That's one small step for man, one giant leap for mankind."

Since a good portion of the Colorado Plateau in northern Arizona bears a strong resemblance to moonscape, NASA decided to use it as a training ground for the Apollo astronauts. The Grand Canyon provided a veritable textbook, each layer a page in geological time. From 1963 until 1972, fifty astronauts—including all twelve who walked on the moon—took part in thirty-seven different training exercises at sites that included the Grand Canyon, Barringer Meteoric Crater ("Meteor Crater"), Sunset Crater, the Hopi Buttes, and Merriam Crater. In 1969, near Sunset Crater, two crater fields were blasted into the earth using explosives. Within a year, a winter training site was constructed near Cottonwood in the Verde Valley.

At places like Meteor Crater, astronauts rode vehicles on the lunar-like surface and learned to tell the difference between meteorite craters and volcanic craters, a distinction that had eluded scientists for centuries. Meteor Crater, the largest and best-preserved crater on earth, was believed to be a volcanic steam crater from the time it was discovered in 1871 until 1959. The crater is 570 feet deep and nearly a mile across with a lip some 150 feet high. It is named for Daniel Moreau Barringer, a Philadelphia lawyer who believed that, with all the meteorite fragments laying around, a fortune in nickel-iron must lie beneath the surface at the bottom of the crater, and he spent $600,000 in a futile search for it.

The man who masterminded the training sites for the Apollo Space Program was renowned geologist-astronomer Gene Shoemaker. A graduate of the California Institute of Technology, he first became interested in the study of the moon in 1948 while working for the U.S. Geological Survey in Navada. A visit to Meteor Crater in 1952 convinced him that both it and the lunar craters were due to asteroidal impacts. In 1957 he began investigating the crater and made an interesting discovery. In one of Dan Barringer's old drill shafts, he found a level of broken rock and, below that, shattered and fused rock. His study of this rock, which prompted scientists to re-think their theories on craters—both lunar and terrestrial—solidified Shoemaker as the founder of the science of impact geology.

In 1960, Shoemaker received his doctorate from Princeton with a thesis on Meteor Crater. A year later he took a leading role in the U.S.G.S. program in Flagstaff, where he coined the phrase "astrogeology." The venture included the mapping of the moon, the Ranger missions to the moon, and the training of the astronauts. Addison's disease prevented Shoemaker from realizing his dream of becoming an astronaut, but in 1965 he was named chief scientist at the U.S.G.S. Center of Astrogeology in Flagstaff.

John Young (front) and Charles Duke (back), Apollo 16 lunar astronauts field training on Lunar Rover Vehicle northeast of Flagstaff.

Astrogeologist Gerald Schaber of Flagstaff was involved in the training programs for the Apollo astronauts and is the only remaining member of the Apollo Lunar Surface Geologic Team still active with the U.S.G.S. Schaber joined the program in July 1965, and today provides a link to a relatively unknown but important part of the Apollo program.

To be sure, many stories came from the training of astronauts in Northern Arizona. The following yarn is certainly one of the most enlightening. One day while they were out practicing maneuvers, an old Navajo medicine man was seen curiously watching the proceedings from a nearby hill. Finally he strolled down and approached a couple of well-dressed, urban-looking Navajo men, generally referred to by the more traditional Navajo as "gray suits." He asked what was going on.

The old man didn't speak English, so they conversed in the native language. "These men will be the first people from earth to set foot on the moon," they told the medicine man, who shook his head. "That's not so," he corrected. "A long time ago some of Our People left the earth on a journey to the sun and, on their way, stopped off at the moon."

When the gray suits translated what the old man said, NASA officials decided it would make a great media story. They asked if the old man would agree to speak into a tape recorder and give a message for the astronauts to take along and pass on to any Navajo who might still be on the moon.

The old man agreed to pass along a few words of wisdom to his brothers on the moon. He spoke into the tape recorder in his native tongue. Afterward, the NASA people could hardly contain their curiosity. "What did he say?" they anxiously asked one of the gray suits.

"Don't make any treaties with these guys," one replied laconically.

Neil Armstrong at the Grand Canyon.

THE ME DECADE

"I can categorically say that no one on the present White House staff, no one in this administration, was involved in this very bizarre incident."

—Richard Nixon, responding to questions on the Watergate break-in

"There are so many lies you can take, and now there has been one too many. Nixon should get his ass out of the White House today."

—Senator Barry Goldwater, 1974

WRITER TOM WOLFE called the 1970s the "Me Decade," and the appellation stuck. In an essay from this work, Wolfe, one of the most important writers of the decade, theorized the "Third Great Awakening." Following three decades of prosperity, Americans had more time and money to focus on "me." The path of happiness was self-indulgence. Some went for self-awareness, but it always began with "me."

Trying to get in touch with ourselves, we shared our most intimate thoughts with encounter groups. We got in touch and decided we were mostly okay. Bumper stickers and T-shirts proclaimed, "I'm OK, You're OK." It was the mantra of a society trying to prop itself up. Yellow Smiley Faces were pasted everywhere. People flashed saccharine smiles and chortled, "Have a nice day." It was enough to make one want to go out and intentionally have a bad day.

The seventies conjure up images of bell-bottom jeans, Nehru jackets, and polyester leisure suits. Women were still burning their bras and demanding revolutionary shifts in attitudes and laws having to do with age-old structures they felt were discriminatory. Baby boomers believed they could change the world. The media made celebrities of the most outrageous leaders of the youth movement, thus encouraging even more outrageous behavior and violence.

By 1970 public opinion had turned against the war in Vietnam. Many protesters were college students, able to afford ways to avoid the draft, while many blue-collar workers saw their sons being drafted and sent to Vietnam. Campus unrest peaked in the early seventies. In response, protesting construction workers waving American flags held "hard-hat rallies." They attacked student protesters, whom they referred to derisively as "long hairs."

Americans were moving further out into the "burbs." Social psychologists called it "White Flight." Suburbia was the new frontier, where settlers flocked to find a new life. They staked out their claims on sixty-by-forty lots.

The automobile, it was said, accounted for suburbia, and suburbia accounted for the shopping mall. Shopping malls, like suburbs, were spreading across the countryside like fungi. By the mid-1970s there were fifteen thousand shopping malls in America.

Senator McCain greets
President Nixon.

Watergate's Web

IN POLITICS, after an overwhelming victory over Senator George McGovern in the presidential election of 1972, the downfall of Richard Nixon was swift. Earlier that year, on June 17, 1972, five burglars were arrested in the Democratic National Headquarters at the Watergate office building in Washington. Their subsequent identification as hirelings of the Re-elect the President group began the long, drawn-out Watergate Affair. What unfolded was the greatest political crisis in U.S. history. Nixon denied any involvement but evidence proved otherwise. Under threat of impeachment for obstruction of justice, he resigned on August 8, 1974. House Majority Leader John Rhodes and Senator Barry Goldwater comprised two of the three men who went to Richard Nixon and persuaded him to resign.

Among the tragic figures caught in Nixon's web was attorney general Richard Kleindienst. A longtime Arizonan, he was an unsuccessful candidate for governor in 1964, losing in the general election to Sam

Goddard. A solid Republican party organizer, he'd been instrumental in lining up delegates for Goldwater's nomination in 1964 and had led the efforts to encourage Nixon to run in 1968. Kleindienst, an astute, experienced politician, had been appointed attorney general by Nixon just before the Watergate scandal broke. Kleindienst quickly found himself in a hornet's nest. Barry Goldwater, in his book, *With No Apologies,* insisted Kleindienst would never have allowed such shenanigans had he been in office at the time. "Kleindienst," said Goldwater, "had not been involved with Watergate or any other impropriety." Still, he was forced to resign and face charges along with others in the Nixon administration.

Post-Watergate Blues

AFTER WATERGATE, the nation struggled to regain equilibrium and restore some lost faith. A period of introspection began. Vice President Gerald Ford ascended to the presidency. He was a good man, plainspoken and earnest, but he didn't inspire. Once, during a speech before Congress, opposition party leader Carl Albert was caught on television dozing off. Ford's jokes were wooden, and many Americans felt betrayed and outraged when he pardoned Richard Nixon a month after the president resigned in dishonor. When inflation got out of control, the former Michigan football player encouraged Americans to wear WIN (Whip Inflation Now) buttons on their clothing as if some cheerleading slogan would defeat runaway inflation.

After the buffoonish Jerry Ford, Americans were treated to Jimmy Carter's piney-woods, born-again testimony that made everyone feel guilty for sinning even if it was only in their hearts.

Technology and Medicine

HISTORICALLY, Arizona was on the cutting edge of new medical advances. The frontier gave doctors an opportunity to perform experimental surgery. They didn't have the same restraints as their Eastern colleagues. They weren't subject to medical boards and review and could improvise at will. If the patient survived the ordeal, the doctor wrote a paper on it. On the other hand, if the patient didn't survive, no one was the wiser.

Tombstone's famous "gunshot physician," Dr. George Goodfellow, wrote numerous articles on the treatment of gunshot wounds. He also performed the first perineal prostatectomy in the nation and was one of the first to perform an appendectomy.

Times changed in the twentieth century, but Arizona remained on the cutting edge. In 1971 Dr. Edward B. Diethrich of Phoenix, an internationally renowned cardiovascular surgeon, founded the Arizona Heart Institute, the nation's first freestanding outpatient clinic devoted solely to the prevention, detection, and treatment of heart and blood vessel diseases.

In 1971 the Heart Institute became the first to use treadmill testing in Arizona. In 1983 Dr. Diethrich, sometimes referred locally to as "Ted Terrific," performed the first live telecast of open-heart surgery on prime-time television. Four years later he was the first to use laser technology during coronary artery bypass surgery. In 1988 he performed Arizona's first coronary stent procedure (the insertion of a tiny screen into the clogged artery to keep it open), and in 1994 the first outpatient coronary stent in the United States. Three years later, he performed the first implantation of a Schneider wall graft endoprosthesis in the world.

The Changing of the Guard

IN THE FIRST FORTY YEARS following statehood the Democrats controlled the legislature. Facing little opposition from Republicans, they broke into factions, something that caused one political wag to comment, "Arizona has three political parties: Democrats, Democrats, and Republicans." Liberal or moderate Democrat governors were constantly at odds with conservative Democrats in the legislature, who formed coalitions with Republicans.

By the seventies, registered Republicans and Democrats in Arizona had equalized in numbers. For Republicans it had been a long journey.

In 1942 and 1944 more than 87 percent of the voters registered as Democrats. The Eisenhower landslide in the fifties helped narrow the gap, as did the immigration of Republican Midwesterners to Arizona. Also important was the influence of outstanding Republicans such as Barry Goldwater, Howard Pyle, John Rhodes, Paul Fannin, and Jack Williams. They increased the party's popularity, and many conservative Democrats in the state came to identify with Republican ideology.

John Rhodes.

One plainspoken old Democrat stalwart saw it all in a different light. "We didn't have any damn Republicans in Arizona," he lamented, "until we got air conditioning."

Arizona saw many changes in the governor's office during the decade. The seventies began with longtime radio personality and Phoenix mayor Jack Williams at the helm. He retired in 1974. His successor was former judge and foreign ambassador, Raul Castro. Castro was the state's first Hispanic chief executive. He left office before his term expired to accept another ambassadorial appointment and was replaced by secretary of state Wesley Bolin. Bolin died a few months after taking office, and since the current secretary of state, Rose Mofford, had been appointed rather than elected, the next in line, attorney general Bruce Babbitt, ascended to the governor's office.

A Christmas Tragedy

ON DECEMBER 19, 1970, around midnight, a Christmas party was in full swing in the ballroom at the historic Pioneer Hotel in Tucson. Two floors above, an arsonist was at work. Suddenly smoke and flames engulfed the eleven-story building. The fire turned into an inferno, moving up the stairs at an incredible speed. Twenty-nine people perished in the fire. Lewis Taylor, a fifteen-year-old boy with a juvenile record, was arrested and convicted for the crime and sentenced to life in prison.

Organized Crime

ARIZONA HAD GAINED A REPUTATION in the nineteenth century as a rough-and-tumble land of desperadoes. The state had a hard time living down that reputation. Outlaws were the stuff of storybooks and movies, hard-riding men who held up stagecoaches and trains or rode into town and robbed banks. More sophisticated, modern Mafia and mob criminal activity was believed to be confined to Chicago or New York, and during the fifties politicians indignantly denied the activities of mobs in Arizona. Despite the denial, the mob was here, albeit keeping a low profile. Back East, mobs were able to control many unions. Since Arizona was a right-to-work state, unions were weak.

Gus Greenbaum and Willie Bioff were among those living in the state who were victims of mob hits in 1958. During the 1960s, Ned Warren earned himself the dubious title Godfather of Land Scams for his shady real-estate dealings. Later, he was tried, convicted, and sent to prison, where he died a few years later of natural causes.

Arizona officials were still in denial about organized crime when *Arizona Republic* reporter Don Bolles was killed in a car bombing in June 1976. Although the prosecution couldn't prove mob involvement, the murder shocked Arizonans and brought national media attention to the state. John Harvey Adamson admitted he lured Bolles to the Clarendon House in Phoenix and placed six sticks of dynamite under his car, then exploded them with a remote control radio device. He turned state's evidence, accusing a contractor named Max Dunlap of hiring him and James Robison, a Chandler plumber, to kill Bolles. Both were convicted and sentenced to death. Both were eventually granted a new trial. Robison's conviction was reversed, while Dunlap was found guilty again and is currently behind bars. The exact details and truth behind the murder of Bolles remains a mystery.

The Tison Gang

ONE OF THE GREATEST manhunts in Arizona history occurred in 1978. On July 30, convicted killers Gary Tison and Randy Greenawalt broke out of the state prison at Florence using guns smuggled in by Tison's three sons, Donald, Ricky, and Raymond. At the time of the escape, Gary Tison was serving a life sentence for killing a prison guard in 1967 while he was in prison for embezzlement. In 1974 Randy Greenawalt murdered a truck driver near Flagstaff in cold blood.

The so-called Tison Gang then went on a twelve-day rampage that began near Quartzsite and ended in a bloody gun battle near Casa Grande. The terror began a day after the escape. The gang had a flat tire and flagged down a passing motorist, Marine sergeant, John Lyons. With Lyons was his wife, their twenty-two-month-old baby and a fifteen-year-old niece, Teresa Tyson. The family was abducted, driven to a secluded spot, and murdered with shotguns. Ironically, the site of the murder was a place called Tyson Wash.

A few days later the gang murdered a honeymooning couple in southern Colorado and stole their van. They headed back into Arizona and eventually to Casa Grande, where the Tisons lived. On August 10, a Casa Grande police officer followed the van momentarily. Inside the van, the gang had him in their gun sights and were about to shoot when the officer turned down a side street.

On August 11, the Tison gang tried to crash their stolen van into a roadblock near Casa Grande. During the ten-minute gunfight, Gary Tison escaped into the desert, where he died of exposure. His body was found eleven days later, about a mile from the site of the gunfight.

During the firefight, Donald took a bullet in the forehead and died instantly, while Greenawalt and the two other Tison boys were captured and later convicted of the murders near Quartzsite.

Greenawalt was executed at the state prison on January 23, 1997. Ricky and Raymond Tison were given the death sentence but were granted a new trial and are currently serving life sentences.

Thieves of Time

IN 1979 A new federal law, the Archaeological Resources Protection Act, expanded efforts to deal with pot hunters. The new law carried a possible $10,000 fine and a year in prison for the first offense and up to a $100,000 fine and five years in prison for subsequent offenses. Along with that, the offender's vehicle could be confiscated. The law also went after buyers and sellers of illegal artifacts. Previously, offenders felt their crimes were worth the risk because the value of the artifacts far outweighed the fines. Lawmen were not highly motivated because of the relatively minor penalties. The new law gave violators something to think about, and even more to think about when the fines were later increased to $250,000.

There is much still to be learned from Arizona's ancient cultures, but the systematic looting of prehistoric sites for their commercial value by individuals who are fully aware of the impact and illegality of their acts robs us of this knowledge. They are, in the words of writer Tony Hillerman, "thieves of time."

Mo Udall, Funny Man

IN POLITICS Arizona's Morris "Mo" Udall made a valiant attempt to win the Democratic nomination before losing to Jimmy Carter in the campaign of 1976. He later wrote a delightful best-selling book titled *Too Funny to Be President.*

During his career in Washington, Udall's self-deprecating good humor defused many a tense political situation and won him much acclaim. But he had his serious side, too. He was a strong advocate for environmental protection. In 1984, he was named the most respected and effective member of the U.S. Congress.

Udall was born and raised in the small town of St. Johns. He used to say, "I come from St. Johns, a town so small, I was in the fifth grade before I knew the town's name wasn't Resume Speed."

Mo Udall and his brother Stewart starred for the University of Arizona basketball team. In 1948–49, while attending law school, Mo played for the Denver Nuggets in the old National Basketball League. His salary was a lofty $8,000 a season. He'd learned to fly, and on trips he sometimes filled in for the pilot flying the team plane, an old, run-down DC-3. How many other ex-professional athletes can make that claim? The team did badly and the owner went broke. Udall never did get paid. However, the owner presented him with a stock certificate worth $10,000. Udall later mused that the certificate "is as valueless today as it was then."

After graduating from law school Mo Udall began practicing law in Tucson. In 1961, after President Kennedy appointed his brother Stewart as secretary of the interior, Mo won a special election and went off to Washington to represent Arizona's second Congressional District.

Morris Udall.

Udall tells of a time, during his race for the presidential nomination, when his car got stuck in the snow in New Hampshire and he decided to do a little ad-lib campaigning. He stuck his head in the door of a small barber shop and announced, "Mo Udall, I'm running for president."

The barber replied, "Yeah, I know. We were laughing about it just this morning."

HAVING IT ALL

"I'm not a racist. I've got black friends. I employ black people. I don't employ them because they're black. I employ them because they are the best people for the cotton-picking job."

—Evan Mecham, January 1987

THE EIGHTIES BEGAN with a volcano and ended with a crumbling wall. On May 18, 1980, Mount St. Helens erupted, spewing ash all over the Pacific northwest. Nearly a decade later, on November 9, 1989, the Berlin Wall came tumbling down. The "Evil Empire" had crumbled. The war against Communism was won. Trying to keep up with the U.S. finally wore Russia down. The Star Wars technology officially known as Strategic Defense Initiative (SDI) was the final straw. As America made serious preparations for a new generation of technology, the Russians, their economy in shambles, threw in the towel. America outlasted 'em, pure and simple. It was a decade that saw socialism fall from grace not only in East bloc countries but also in France, Spain, and England.

Watchwords of the eighties included CD (compact disc), computer virus, couch potato, crack cocaine, fax, Glasnost, gridlock, high five, laptops, Lyme's disease, microwavable, PCs, and spreadsheets.

In the world of fashion, the trendy color was black. Women opted for comfort over chic. Running shoes were in, as were acid-washed denim jeans. The eighties saw a return of the miniskirt. People started drinking less Jack Daniels and more chardonnay. Health-food stores and fitness emporiums flourished. A health-conscious, calorie-conscious populace embraced such delicacies as oat bran, bottled water, light beer, and nonfat foods. Losing weight became a national obsession. Liposuction was the most-requested plastic surgery.

The eighties were all about having it all. For some, having it all wasn't all that good. In 1981 scientists identified Acquired Immune Deficiency Syndrome (AIDS).

Yuppies, Buppies, and Dinks

THE EIGHTIES was a decade of endless talk shows, music videos on television, and video cassette rental stores. Lotteries became popular as a remedy for that irresistible urge to find an easy way to get rich without working. Flower children grew up to be mommies and daddies of conservative children.

Baby boomers came of age and moved into power positions in industry. Hippies and dope heads of the sixties grew up and became stock brokers. The don't-trust-anyone-over-thirty group was now over thirty. The whining and complaining of affluent, self-obsessed boomer subspecies like yuppies, buppies, and dinks reached a peak in the eighties and commanded an inordinate amount of media attention. Having 2.2 children became as trendy as attending aerobics classes. Retailers licked their chops and provided children's designer clothes, jogging strollers, and minivans for soccer moms.

There were very few artistic leaps worth remembering. The best thing that can be said about rap music is that it was original. Movie taste for the eighties is perhaps best illustrated by the 1980 horror flick *Friday the 13th*. By the end of the decade, seven sequels had been imposed upon the public. Jason would prove to be harder to get rid of than Evan Mecham.

Country music became more popular than ever. The seventies "outlaw" music of Waylon and Willie gave way to onstage pyrotechnics and "hat acts," so called because of the high-crown, wide-brim cowboy hats worn by such luminaries as George Strait and Garth Brooks.

People "cocooned," or as they used to say in the Old West, they "holed up." The epidemic of sexually transmitted diseases, nature's payoff for the free-love sixties and seventies, slowed club-hopping and casual sex. Yuppies sought other types of entertainment, such as Trivial Pursuit and jogging. The best example of the new lifestyle of making "honest women" out of live-in girlfriends was the marriage of Playboy Hugh Hefner to one of his Bunnies.

There was a high-tech explosion of fax machines, personal computers, personal stereos for jogging and exercise, answering machines, VCRs, compact disc players, microwave ovens, and pagers. Digital restoration of recordings was introduced in 1987. The songs rerecorded from those old seventy-eights never sounded so good.

Arizona continued to lead the way in medical breakthroughs. The CBS news program *48 Hours* featured a cardiac standstill procedure, perfected at Barrow Neurological Institute in Phoenix by Dr. Robert F. Spetzler. During this procedure, the heart is stopped and the patient's temperature is lowered by forty degrees, allowing surgeons to drain the blood from the head in order to reach tiny blood vessels and make repairs. Dangerous aneurysms previously considered inoperable could now be treated successfully by putting the patient into "suspended animation" during neurosurgery.

Other medical news during the decade included Pope John Paul's visit to St. Joseph's Hospital and Medical Center in 1987. The Phoenix hospital was the only one the Pope visited during his ten-day tour of the U.S. One of the major themes of the well-publicized tour was the health care mission of the Catholic Church.

In 1988 former First Lady Nancy Reagan dedicated the Dr. Loyal and Edith Davis Neurological Research Laboratory in honor of her parents, longtime Arizona residents.

And a year later, Barrow Neurological Institute received national acclaim once more when doctors reattached the spine and skull of a Glendale youngster who'd been critically injured in a truck-bicycle accident.

Another Arizona First

IN THE EIGHTIES, Arizonans were again making news on the national scene. On July 7, 1981, President Ronald Reagan nominated Sandra Day O'Connor to the U.S. Supreme Court. She would be the first woman appointed to the supreme court of the land. O'Connor was the granddaughter of Henry Clay Day, a pioneer rancher in Greenlee County. The historic Lazy B was in her family for more than a century.

She gave up her earlier dreams of becoming a cattle rancher and attended law school at Stanford instead. There she met and eventually married classmate John O'Connor. Returning to Arizona in 1957, she practiced law and became active in civic affairs. From 1969 to 1975 she served in the state legislature. In 1973 she was elected senate majority leader, the first woman in the nation to hold that position. Before her appointment to the high court she was a superior court and court of appeals judge. She took her seat on the Supreme Court (which included class-

Sandra Day O'Connor at the Lazy B Ranch.

mate William Rehnquist, another Arizonan) in October 1981.

Although O'Connor graduated in the top 10 percent of her law class at Stanford in 1952, she was unable to hire on with a law firm in California. The bias against women attorneys at the time was such that she later commented, "They had never hired a woman. I was offered a job as secretary—provided I could type well."

Bruce Babbitt

BRUCE BABBITT, scion of the legendary family of entrepreneurs, merchants, and ranchers in the Flagstaff area, served as governor from 1978 to 1986. The four Babbitt brothers, David, Billy, George, and Charles J., began the CO Bar ranch, named for their hometown of Cincinatti, Ohio, in 1886. They started with a grubstake of less than $20,000 and built it into one of the state's greatest family dynasties. In 1889 the

Babbitt Brothers Trading Company in downtown Flagstaff.

Babbitt Brothers Trading Company was established, and soon the outfit dominated economics in northern Arizona. Bruce is the grandson of Charles J. Babbitt.

After graduating from Harvard Law School in 1967, he became active in the civil rights movement in the South. Afterward he returned to Arizona and went into law practice. He entered politics for the first time in 1974, running for the office of state attorney general. When Wesley Bolin died in office in early 1978, the elected secretary of state was to become governor by law. However, since Rose Mofford had filled the position by appointment when Bolin assumed the governor's office, the attorney general was legally next in line. Babbitt, who'd been contemplating running for the U.S. Senate, became governor.

Thoughtful and intelligent, Babbitt was arguably one of the best governors in the state's history. He elevated the

Bruce Babbitt.

office to one of high profile. He worked well with the Republican-controlled legislature and earned respect on both sides of the aisle.

After leaving the governor's office, Babbitt made an unsuccessful run for the Democratic nomination for president in 1988. Coming from a small state like Arizona was a major problem and his campaign fizzled during the early primaries. He did, however, gain much national respect and attention. When Bill Clinton was elected president in 1992, Babbitt was appointed secretary of the interior.

Speculation ran high during the mid-1990s that Babbitt would be appointed to fill a vacancy on the U.S. Supreme Court, making him the third Arizonan on the court. However, President Clinton considered Babbitt's role as secretary of the interior too critical at the time.

Arizona Teams and Coaches

THE BIGGEST Arizona sports story of the decade was the NFL St. Louis Cardinals' move to the state in 1988. (Originally called the Phoenix Cardinals, the name was later changed to the Arizona Cardinals for a state-wide identity.) Actually, the Cards weren't the first professional football team in Arizona. A couple of teams in the sixties and seventies might qualify. Also, in 1983, the Arizona Wranglers played in the short-

Phoenix Cardinals v. Washington Redskins.

lived USFL. Two years later they changed their name to the Outlaws.

For a time, the Outlaws were coached by the legendary Frank Kush, who coached the ASU Sun Devils from 1958 to 1979 during the golden years of ASU sports. Over twenty-two seasons Kush compiled a record of 176 wins, with only 54 losses. He later coached in the Canadian Football League and the National Football League. A tough, hard-nosed native of a Pennsylvania coal mining town, Kush was a 175-pound All-American guard during his years at Michigan State.

Arizona State University was blessed with some of the nation's greatest coaches during the golden years, including Bobby Winkles and Jim Brock in baseball, Ned Wulk in basketball, and Senon "Baldy" Castillo in track. The list of football coaches, including assistants, looks like a "who's who." Among them were Kush, Dan Devine, Cecil Coleman, Dick Tamburo, Al Onofrio, and Chuck Fairbanks. All had illustrious careers in both college and professional ranks.

The next big sports story of the eighties was the Sun Devils' 22-15 victory over Michigan in the 1987 Rose Bowl. They finished the season ranked fourth in the nation with a 10-1-1 record.

The University of Arizona Wildcat basketball team electrified fans all over the state during the 1987–88 season. Sean Elliott, Steve Kerr, Anthony Cook, and Tom Tolbert led the team to a number-one ranking and to the NCAA Final Four. All went on to play in the National Basketball Association. Another member of the team, Kenny Lofton, went on to play major league baseball.

Something ASU fans would like to forget was the way their chief nemesis and spoiler, the University of Arizona Wildcats, completely dominated the Sun Devils during the decade. During that span the Sun Devils went eight years without a victory—they beat U of A only twice in ten games.

Still Growing

AS IN DECADES PAST, Arizona's population growth overshadowed everything else. The population grew from 1.7 million in 1970 to 2.7 million

THE END OF THE MOTHER ROAD

In 1984 fabled Route 66 was declared officially dead when the last stretch of freeway bypassed the town of Williams. The highway, dubbed the Mother Road by John Steinbeck, began its demise in 1956, when America's interstate highway system kicked in. The 376-mile journey across northern Arizona, originally the National Old Trail Highway, followed the historic Beale camel survey of the 1850s and the Santa Fe railroad of the early 1880s. With the advent of the automobile came the demand for better transcontinental highways. In 1922 the National Old Trail Highway was graded along the route of the Santa Fe railroad. In 1926 it was renamed U.S. Route 66. Paving of the road was completed in 1938.

The storied highway was the subject of songs like "(Get Your Kicks On) Route 66" and a television series in the 1950s called Route 66. The Mother Road will never really die as long as folks like Seligman's colorful Route 66 promoter, Angel Delgadillo, are around to keep its spirit alive. His ice cream parlor is a gathering spot for those pilgrims wanting to take a sentimental journey through places with names like Hackberry and Peach Springs.

Ash Fork, Arizona, 1980.

in 1980. By the end of the decade it had risen another million. Arizona had the second-highest growth percentage in the nation, 37.6; only Nevada's 47.4 was higher. During the eighties the Phoenix metropolitan area grew from 1.5 million to 1.9 million. Nearly 60 percent of the state's residents lived in Maricopa County. Ironically, the population actually declined 3 percent in the late eighties, a drop that could be attributed mostly to an economic downturn.

In 1980 the legislature adopted an underground water management code. In 1984, after some sixty years of struggle, the long-awaited Central Arizona Project began delivering water to the Salt River Valley. A few years later, it reached its final destination at Tucson.

Freeway construction in Phoenix, delayed in the 1970s by those who felt the Papago freeway would divide the city, was approved for construction in 1982. Three years later voters approved a twenty-year, half-cent sales tax to finance over two hundred more miles of freeway in the Valley.

Arizonans have long differed on the issue of mass transportation and building freeways. The sprawling area is thought by many to be unsuitable for mass transportation, yet the streets and freeways are, at times, on the verge of gridlock. In spring of 1989, voters again had an opportunity to demonstrate a vision of the future by voting for a plan called Val Trans. Val Trans called for, among other things, a rapid transit rail

Modern downtown Phoenix.

ARIZONA 2000

system throughout the Valley. Like the Rio Salado Project that called for developing lands along the Salt River, voters turned it down, claiming it was too expensive. The results left visionaries asking the question, "Where do we go from here?"

Hard Times for Miners

SINCE THE EARLY 1900S, Arizona had been the nation's leader in copper production. During the Cold War years, the state produced more of the red metal than the rest of the free world combined. But by the 1980s much of the world's copper was being mined overseas. On the world market, copper declined from $1.45 a pound to a low of 61 cents. Competition from foreign markets, along with higher labor costs, was causing copper companies to lose money. When union contracts expired, Phelps Dodge, the state's leading copper producer, took a hard line in the negotiations with labor. The result was a year-long strike at the Clifton-Morenci mines in July 1983. It was 1903 all over again.

Fear of violence by striking miners led Governor Bruce Babbitt to send National Guard troops and Department of Public Safety officers to the area to keep the peace. In the end, the company succeed in busting the union, much the same as they had done in Bisbee in 1917. By the end of the decade, the number of copper miners in the state had dropped from some 21,000 to 12,100.

Humpty-Dumpty

FOR YEARS, it was boom times for real estate and construction in the state. But by 1988, economists were predicting a collapse. The area was overbuilt and overextended. The first of the large firms to fall was Western Savings, a solid company that had been around since the 1920s. Then it was learned that Pinnacle West Capital Corporation, the holding company for both Mera Bank and Arizona Public Service, was in financial trouble. Such solid old banking institutions as First Interstate

THE MAKING OF MECHAM

✳ Evan Mecham was one of the most interesting and controversial politicians in Arizona history. He had a solid core of devout followers and was always a politician to be reckoned with. To better understand the Mecham years, it helps to get some insight into what made Evan Mecham.

He was born and raised in a small, rural Mormon community in Utah, where there were no blacks or homosexuals, and a woman's place was in the home rearing children. He went off to World War II, was shot down over Germany, and spent the last few months of the war in a prison camp. He came home after the war and settled in Glendale, where he'd trained as a combat pilot at Luke Air Force Base. He opened up a successful Pontiac dealership and began to participate in politics.

In 1960 he was elected to the Arizona Senate. Two years later he ran and lost against Carl Hayden for the U.S. Senate. With strong backing from ultraright-wing conservatives, he ran in the Republican primary for governor in 1964, but lost to Richard Kleindienst by a margin of two to one. The bitter personal attacks that became Mecham's trademark contributed to Kleindienst's loss to Democrat Sam Goddard. Undaunted, Mecham lashed out at party leaders, further enhancing his reputation as a maverick. He ran unsuccessfully for governor in 1974, 1978, and again in 1982 before finally grabbing the brass ring in 1986. Mecham saw his miracle victory as divinely inspired. He would save Arizona from embracing socialism. His strong religious faith would see him through this "trial by fire."

(First National Bank of Arizona) and Valley National Bank were shaken to their foundations.

The biggest fall was yet to come. For years the sprawling financial empire of Charles Keating, Jr. had epitomized the boom times in the state. He was like a kind old uncle, donating vast sums of money to good causes. He'd built a plush, Taj Mahal–like resort on the side of Camelback Mountain and did radio spots espousing family values, Mom, and apple pie. Suddenly, on April 13, 1989, his real-estate development firm, American Continental Corporation, filed for bankruptcy protection. Federal prosecutors charged Keating and his associates in a $1.1 billion racketeering lawsuit that has been called the largest in U.S. history. Keating was convicted and did jail time, but the conviction was overturned.

The Mecham Years

IN 1986 an odd turn of events created one of the most chaotic periods in Arizona's political history. Entrepreneur Bill Schulz had made a surprisingly strong run for Barry Goldwater's senate seat in 1982, barely losing. With his credibility as a viable candidate established, he was the front-runner in the race for governor in 1986. Suddenly, he pulled out of the race.

On the Republican side, state representative Burton Barr, one of the state's most powerful politicians, seemed to be a shoo-in for the nomination. Then a strange thing happened. Evan Mecham, a Glendale car dealer and perennial candidate, pulled a stunning upset in the primary, defeating Barr.

The longtime superintendent of public instruction, Carolyn Warner, won the Democratic

Evan Mecham.

nomination. Many were unhappy with the choice of candidates, and this prompted Schulz to reenter the race as an independent. At first it looked as if Schulz had the magic to win the governorship, but his campaign fizzled at the end and he took enough votes away from Warner to hand the election to Mecham.

Mecham, an ultraconservative, won the office on his fifth try. He was a feisty and strong-willed man who proudly claimed he was not a professional politician. Many Arizonans, especially those in rural areas, saw Mecham as a man who stood up for the little guy, a man who would root out corruption and rid the state of the "ruling elite," the power brokers and nabobs who held sway over state affairs. Mecham enthusiastically prepared to impose his programs for reforming state government. He declared war on drugs and crime. A fiscal conservative and businessman, many of his cost-cutting measures were sound. He was applauded for stopping the practice of allowing some state employees to drive state cars to and from work. He seemed the man fit for the times.

Mecham's populist rhetoric sounded good, but he quickly learned that in government things are easier said than done. He and his administration came into office with a strong mistrust for the traditional way government agencies operated. Mecham and his staff stubbornly refused to seek help or accept help from state agencies, the legislature, or the attorney general. Mecham's inability to work with the Republican-dominated legislature turned what should have been an amicable relationship into all-out war. He cut off lines of communication with all who disagreed with him, vetoed bills if the sponsor had done something to offend him, and failed to consult with GOP leaders on key decisions.

Another problem that plagued the Mecham administration concerned the qualifications of a number of key appointees. Critics claimed many were chosen by old-fashioned cronyism or that he picked those of his ideological persuasion. Many appointees didn't even meet minimum qualifications, but Mecham stubbornly insisted they be hired anyway.

In the months that followed, Mecham began to accuse his detractors of being part of a plot by organized crime, in cooperation with the "establishment," to depose him. Attorney general Bob Corbin was accused of spying on Mecham's office from his office with some kind of

Buck Rogers, laser-beaming device. Mecham's enemies list grew from a "few dissident Democrats and homosexuals" to include most of the state legislature, the head of the Department of Public Safety, Attorney General Bob Corbin, the media, and anyone else who criticized him.

Had Mecham's personal style been less offensive—had he spent some time in the Ronald Reagan charm school—his reform program might have been better received. Mecham would later say, "I guess they just don't like my politics."

He made himself readily available to the media, and they never went away from an interview without something quotable. The problem was it nearly always made him come out looking bad. He referred to blacks as lovable "pickanninies." He joked how some Asians' eyes got "round" on hearing good news. Along the way he also offended Hispanics, women, and Jews.

His first act as governor, rescinding the Martin Luther King, Jr. holiday, got him in the deepest trouble. The holiday may or may not have been created legally by his predecessor, Bruce Babbitt, and Mecham could have declared it illegal on those grounds. But he chose to expound on the subject, and the media had a heyday. He claimed Dr. King didn't deserve a holiday, a statement that brought national attention to the state. The tourism business collectively shuddered as corporations began to cancel conventions in Arizona.

Within months of his election Mecham found himself facing recall, impeachment, and a criminal trial, something unprecedented in American history at the time. Ironically, he'd campaigned on a platform of honesty, integrity, and lawfulness.

By November 1987, enough signatures were declared valid that a recall election was scheduled for the following May. Then a story broke in the press about a $350,000 campaign loan under investigation by Attorney General Corbin. A few days later, in a separate proceeding, the House hired attorney William French to investigate the charges. In January 1988, Mecham was indicted by the attorney general on six felony charges stemming from the loan, initiating a chain of events that eventually led to his ouster. A week later French reported his findings to the House. Included were two other charges, obstruction of justice and misuse of a protocol fund. Attorneys Paul Eckstein and French acted as prosecutors for the House at the trial, which was presided over by chief justice of the State Supreme Court Frank Gordon.

On April 4, 1988, Mecham was found guilty on two of the three charges. It was the first time in fifty-nine years that a United States governor had been impeached and removed from office. On June 16, a jury found Mecham innocent on charges of violating campaign laws. His detractors claimed it didn't matter; the important thing was that he was out of office. Mecham felt vindicated of any wrongdoing.

Auntie Rose

WHEN MECHAM LEFT OFFICE he was replaced by secretary of state Rose Mofford, an Arizona native from Globe. Mofford, a star softball and basketball player, turned down a chance to play professional basketball to come to Phoenix and work at the capitol. She was a longtime administrative assistant to secretary of state Wesley Bolin. When Bolin succeeded Raul Castro as governor, she was appointed to his old position. She was reelected secretary of state three times and left the governor's office in 1991 after some fifty years of public service.

Mofford will be remembered for her long career of public service, but her greatest legacy will be her handling of the turmoil and ill feelings following the Mecham impeachment. Loved and admired by Democrats and Republicans alike, "Auntie Rose" quickly got rid of the mean-spirited troublemakers who were holdovers from the Mecham administration and began the long, slow healing process.

Rose Mofford.

A MILLENNIUM ENDS

"We think that you all think it is more exciting than we do."

—Governor Jane Dee Hull, commenting to reporters
on the inauguration of five women—
"the Fab Five"—to the top five elective posts in Arizona,
a first in American history.

T HE NINETIES IS A DECADE in search of a definition. The twenties roared; the thirties were depressed; war dominated the forties; the fifties were placid; the sixties were turbulent; the "Me Decade" defined the seventies; and the eighties were referred to as "the Greedy Decade." The epitaph for the nineties has yet to be written.

A defining label could be the "Decade of the Sound Bite," or perhaps the "Politically Correct Decade," or even the "Information Decade." One writer suggested it should be called the "Decade of Anticipation" for the millennium. Author Studs Turkel calls the nineties the "Decade of National Alzheimer's Disease—forgetfulness of yesterday, forgetfulness of history."

The State of the Nation

THE DECADE BEGAN with the end of the Cold War, the war that never was, but tranquility didn't last long. The superpowers were melting swords into plowshares, but outlaw governments around the globe were still a force to be reckoned with. Iraq's tinhorn dictator, Saddam Hussein, opened the decade by invading tiny Kuwait. Operation Desert Storm began January 16, 1991, and by February 28, Iraq's Republican Guards and the rest of the army were routed and running for Bagdad. Unfortunately, an opposing coalition wouldn't destroy Iraq's surviving military power base, and Hussein continued to be a menace and threat to peace in the Middle East.

The nineties were also about communication and information. E-mail, fax machines, and the Web all became a part of our daily lives.

In 1992 the digital cellular phone system was introduced. Ubiquitous car phones distracted drivers and inspired this angry bumper sticker seen on a Phoenix freeway: "Hang up and drive."

Virtual reality was another new wave of the future that has actually been around for awhile. An example is simulated flight training for pilots, used for years. Virtual reality takes real-life simulation to fantastic new levels. The information available through such technology as we approach the next century is best described by another over-used word of the nineties, "awesome."

Arizona's contributions to scientific advancement included medical breakthroughs. During the 1990s, surgeons began using more noninvasive types of surgery. Barrow Neurological Institute (BNI) pioneered gamma knife radiosurgery, a noninvasive, bloodless alternative to neurosurgery. BNI became the test site for this procedure in 1997. Using advanced imaging and three-dimensional computer-planning techniques, surgeons can deliver a single high dose of radiation to destroy a precise target within the brain, while sparing surrounding normal tissue.

BNI gained worldwide attention when a fist-size tumor was successfully removed from a sixteen-year-old boy who was slowly suffocating from the pressure. The youngster's face was disassembled so surgeons could work behind his nasal passage to the base of his brain.

In 1997 BNI doctors used the amazing cardiac standstill procedure to save the life of a five-year-old girl whose skull had been crushed. She was the youngest of sixty-five patients to undergo the procedure since its development the previous decade.

Also in 1997 the Muhammed Ali Parkinson Research Center opened in Phoenix, becoming one of fifty internationally recognized centers for Parkinson's treatment. The former heavyweight champion boxer, who suffers from the disease, plans to help raise funds as an endowment.

Where Have All the Heroes Gone?

IN JULY 1998, Sandy Grady, a Washington columnist for the Philadelphia Daily News, commented on the recent death of astronaut Alan Shepard and how our passion for heroes and great feats had faded. He recalled that morning of May 5, 1961, with Shepard "sitting atop a skinny, frail Redstone rocket" in a doghouse-sized capsule, waiting for four hours while NASA scientists fidgeted with the equipment. (American rockets had a reputation for blowing up like cheap firecrackers.) Finally Shepard growled, "Why don't you fix your little problem and light this candle?"

All America stood still that moment, 9:34 A.M. when, with a blast of flame and a loud "whoosh," the white, pencil-like rocket lifted hesitatingly. Shepard's strong, raspy voice said, "We have a liftoff. The clock is starting." The ungainly projectile tottered, then headed out over the Atlantic, and Americans gave a collective sigh of relief. America had sent her first man into space.

Fast forward to 1998, to what Grady calls the decade of the placid and trivial. "How did we stumble from Alan Shepard's first American space hop," he asks, to a time when "our adrenaline is jolted only by a

VIAGRA AND OTHER MIRACLES

⁂ The 1990s also produced some new miracle drugs. Pharmaceutical companies introduced drugs with purposes that ranged from growing hair to curing impotency. In 1998 a company called Entremed came out with what could be a cancer cure. The drug has proven successful on mice and will soon be ready to be tested on humans. But Viagra, a cure for male impotency, sent shock waves around the world, creating black markets in countries where the drug hasn't been approved.

Viagra jokes made their rounds in the late nineties. Let it suffice to offer just one: On his first honeymoon Paddy Murphy took his bride to Niagara. Forty years later he remarried. This time for the honeymoon, Paddy's bride took him to Viagra.

Dow Jones drop, a meteor-crash movie, or a president's rumored hanky-panky?"

Grady called the early 1960s an age of confidence, challenge, and a reach for glory, tinged with an "ugly darkness beneath the Ozzie and Harriet facade." In other words, the good old days weren't always so good. "What a trade-off!" he writes. "In the nodding '90's we're peacefully prosperous—yet mired in Monica trivia, MTV noise, Windows 98 fads, small-bore politicians, celebrity culture."

The decade of the nineties will also be remembered for an obsession with "political correctness." What began as something noble has gone overboard, creating a nation of people afraid to take a stand on some issue that might be perceived as offensive to somebody, somewhere. Politicians are the worst offenders. Where have you gone, Barry Goldwater?

Homogenized Arizona

ARIZONA HAS BECOME so homogenous in the nineties that it has become as hard to define as the decade itself. The state's population and economic growth continue to rank among the highest in the nation. Recent

Palm tree imports blend with the highrises along Central Avenue in Phoenix.

arrivals to the state say it's easy to fit in because "everybody else is a new-comer, too."

That wasn't always the case. The ethnic heritage of the state is Native American. In the mid-1700s Spanish settlers began arriving from Mexico. The gold rush in the 1860s attracted the whole gamut of frontier society. In the 1870s and 1880s Texan cattlemen drove their herd into Arizona to graze the pristine ranges. During the 1890s hard-rock miners, many of them European immigrants, poured into boom towns like Bisbee, Globe, Clifton, and Jerome. Through it all, the ethnic and geographic personality of the state was pretty easy to define.

In 1900 more than 84 percent of the population lived in rural areas. Ninety years later nearly 88 percent dwell in cities and towns. According to the 1990 census only 37 percent of the population was Arizona born. Some of the old Arizona was still there, but the majority had become part of the sunbelt society: rootless, restless, and in constant flux.

During the second half of the twentieth century, immigrants came to Arizona from a wide range of states, especially those in the East and Midwest. Arizona, like the nation, was becoming more homogenized. There were still a few ethnic neighborhoods left, and a few old families clung tenaciously to farms and ranches, but most residents aspired to reach the American Dream—the good life, a home in suburbia, 2.2 kids, two cars, and a good-paying job. And Arizona was a good place to do it.

During these years Arizona has experienced unprecedented growth, going from a half-million people in 1940 to five million just fifty-five years later. And people keep moving here. Only about 18 percent of the land area in the state is privately owned, so one might ask, "Where are we going to put them?" An old cowboy suggested Arizona would have more land if someone would flatten out the rough places. He claimed that if the state was leveled out, it'd be six times larger than Texas.

Why do they come? In a word, lifestyle. It's a great place to live, work, and play. The Salt River Project Economic Report of 1990 listed the state's positive factors in this order: healthy climate, open spaces, job opportunities, lower living costs, natural beauty, friendliness of the people, abundance of natural resources, good community colleges, and minimum danger of physical hazards such as earthquakes, tornadoes, fires, or floods. It does get a little warm in the summer in the deserts, but remember—it's a dry heat. Don't believe those urban legends about people diving into their swimming pools and getting third-degree burns.

From Trading Posts to Casinos

DURING THE TWENTIETH CENTURY, many native peoples have benefited economically from the land they inherited. In Oklahoma the boon was oil. In other states, it was tourism or minerals, such as coal and copper. In recent years, water rights enriched some tribes. At the Salt River Pima community, much of the land was owned privately by the natives. They leased land along their border with Scottsdale for shopping malls like the Pavilions and other commercial enterprises. A new freeway along that border, negotiated in the early 1990s, was a financial boon to many families.

By far the greatest financial gains have come from the gaming industry. Such tribes as the Yavapai-Apache at Fort McDowell have benefited from gaming casinos, as have others. Some, like the Navajo and Hopi, have resisted the temptation to open casinos on their lands, and this issue has divided people politically. Some see it as a way out of poverty, while others view gambling as a violation of Indian customs and traditions.

Fort McDowell Casino.

The jury is still out on where gaming will take the tribes. The only sure way out of poverty is through education. The Fort McDowell community is setting a good example, pouring much of their revenue back into improving the lives of the people.

Sports Headlines

ARIZONANS WERE AGAIN making sports headlines in the 1990s. During the 1996 Summer Olympic Games, millions of television viewers around the world cheered the courage of Tucson gymnast Kerri Strug. Despite a severe injury to her ankle, Strug nailed her final vault, leading her team to a gold medal.

In March 1997 Lute Olson and his University of Arizona Wildcats brought home the state's first-ever NCAA national basketball championship when they defeated Kentucky 84-79 in the title game. Earlier, on New Year's Day, the Arizona State University football team lost a last-second heartbreaker to Ohio State in the Rose Bowl. The game was their only loss of the season and cost them a national championship.

After a roller-coaster, on-again, off-again Super Bowl, the game was finally played in Arizona at Sun Devil Stadium on January 28, 1996. (The honor of hosting the game had been taken away earlier because the state didn't have a Martin Luther King holiday.) A study showed the game gave the state a three-hundred-million-dollar shot in the economic arm. The NFL then spurned any future Arizona Super Bowls until the state's taxpayers shelled out the money to build a new stadium with enough bells and whistles to be deserving.

Arizona Politics

REPUBLICANS REGAINED CONTROL of the U.S. House in 1994, and among the new breed of young, tax-cutting conservatives elected to go to Washington were Arizonans John Shadegg, Matt Salmon, and J. D. Hayworth.

During the 1990s a few local politicians continued to produce negative headlines. Three years after legislators removed Evan Mecham as governor, some of the same legislators were themselves caught in a sting operation called AzScam. Joseph Stedino, a talk-show host from Las Vegas, worked undercover for the county attorney's office posing as a lobbyist for legalized gambling. He offered bribes to several legislators while hidden video cameras recorded the shameful scene.

The office of governor continued to be troublesome. Real-estate developer Fife Symington III entered office in 1991 after winning a runoff election against Phoenix ex-mayor Terry Goddard. Symington was reelected in 1994, defeating popular Democrat Eddie Basha. Dark clouds began to gather around Symington on June 13, 1996, when he was indicted on twenty-three counts alleging loan fraud and other crimes. This made him the second Arizona governor in less than a decade to face criminal charges.

The charges against Symington had nothing to do with the office of governor but stemmed from loans he arranged as a developer with several lenders to fund his thirty-million-dollar Camelback Esplanade and the ten-million-dollar Mercado development in Phoenix.

Despite his troubles with financing his development projects, Symington was an effective governor and his administration scored high marks. His legacy was one of budget restraint, citizen empowerment, tax relief, and economic restoration. He always stood up for what he believed in and never backed down from a fight, no matter the odds. *Arizona Republic* editorial writer Paul Schatt noted, "He's so tough the cookie dough had to be made of cement with rebar thrown in."

On September 3, 1997, Governor Fife Symington was convicted on seven felony counts and forced from office. Two days later secretary of state Jane Dee Hull was sworn in by Supreme Court justice Sandra Day O'Connor.

In November, the state again made the national news when, for the first time in American history, women were

Governor Jane Dee Hull.

elected to the top five posts in state government, while a sixth was president of the state senate. Arguably, it was the most significant political story of the 1990s. Jane Dee Hull was elected governor (the first woman to be elected governor in the state); Betsey Bayless, secretary of state; Janet Napolitano, attorney general; Carol Springer, treasurer; and Lisa Graham Keegan, superintendent of public instruction. The sixth, Brenda Burns, is president of the state senate. The media quickly dubbed them "the Fab Five," and the group was pictured in *People* magazine. The pop magazine *George* took the hype to the extreme by superimposing the women's faces on the bodies (and wild costumes) of England's rock phoneme, the Spice Girls.

Experienced veterans in public service, the women took it all with good humor and in good stride. It wasn't a "women's movement" or women's block that elected them and they didn't run on women's issues. It also wasn't a political *coup d'etat*. Hull, Bayless, and Keegan were incumbents while Napolitano and Springer weren't running against incumbents. With the exception of Democrat Napolitano, all were Republicans.

In the spirit of working together, Governor Hull unselfishly shared the spotlight on her inauguration day by including the other four in the ceremony. On January 4, 1999, history was made as all five were sworn in by another Arizonan, Supreme Court Justice Sandra Day O'Connor.

The Fab Five, left to right: Janet Napolitano, Lisa Graham Keegan, Carol Springer, Jane Dee Hull, and Betsey Bayless.

The American West during the nineteenth century was a font of opportunity for adventurous women. While magazines of the day extolled the virtues of domesticity and motherhood, they shocked their eastern sisters by straddling horses, driving wagons, mining for gold, and ranching. There were four times as many women lawyers and twice as many women doctors per capita as back East. It was an ideal place for women to express themselves and get back into politics.

Wyoming gave women the vote a half-century before it was granted nationally. By 1924 both Texas and Montana had women governors.

Since statehood, Arizona women have been active in politics. Women's suffrage was granted in 1914, eight years before the Nineteenth Amendment. That same year, Rachel Allen Berry and Frances Willard Munds was the second to serve in a state senate.

Arizona has always held one of the highest percentages of women in state legislatures. In 1999, women comprised 36 percent of the state legislature.

A Rising Political Star

ARIZONA SENATOR JOHN MCCAIN is a man whose star is rising rapidly on the national scene. McCain is the son and grandson of Navy admirals and is a former Navy pilot and ex-POW himself. While flying his twenty-third mission over Vietnam in October 1967, his Skyhawk dive bomber was shot down over Hanoi. He ejected and landed in a downtown lake. His right leg was broken, his left arm was pulled out of its socket, and his right arm was broken in three places. Unconscious, more dead than alive, he was beaten and bayoneted by the North Vietnamese, then thrown into the notorious Hanoi Hilton. He remained a prisoner of war for the next five and a half years, enduring terrible hardships. His hair turned white, and his weight dropped to under a hundred pounds. His broken bones never did mend properly.

Senator John McCain.

Because of his family, the Vietnamese tried to use him for propaganda purposes, but McCain stubbornly refused to cooperate despite the torture inflicted upon him. When the war ended in 1973, he came home and worked as a Navy liaison with the U.S. Senate.

In 1981 he moved to Arizona and the next year ran successfully for Congress. When Goldwater retired in 1986, McCain was the natural choice to succeed him. He's matured very well in Congress and has earned a reputation as a man who puts national interest ahead of parochial or party interests. He was mentioned prominently as Bob Dole's running mate in 1996 and is being touted as presidential timber for the year 2000.

The Passing of Greatness

THE YEAR 1997 saw the passing of Herb Drinkwater, former mayor of Scottsdale and one of the state's most popular politicians. Drinkwater had been active in local politics since the late 1960s, and was mayor for sixteen years before retiring in 1996. Easily recognized by his warm, friendly grin and white cowboy hat, Drinkwater presented the city's grand image as the "West's Most Western Town."

On May 29, 1998 Mr. Arizona, Barry Goldwater, passed away quietly in his home in Paradise Valley. The funeral attracted a legion of politicians from around the country. Congress convened for the funeral and many traveled to Arizona by special plane, attending a ceremony worthy of a chief of state.

Congressman Morris "Mo" Udall passed away on December 12, 1998. Mo Udall was named chairman of the House Interior Committee in 1979, the first Arizonan to hold a House com-

> ✳ *Reflecting on their losses in the bid to become president, Mo Udall said to Barry Goldwater, "Betwen the two of us, we've made Arizona the only state in the Union where mothers don't tell their children they can grow up to be president."*

mittee chair since 1952. Two years later he was diagnosed with Parkinson's disease, which worsened over the years and he resigned from Congress in 1991. President Bill Clinton awarded Udall the Presidential Medal of Freedom, the nation's highest civilian award.

While Goldwater spawned a national political movement, Udall's legacy was sweeping legislation that nearly doubled the nation's parks system, and setting aside 100 million acres of wilderness in Alaska in 1980 with the passage of the 1984 Wilderness Act. This measure set aside more than one million acres in the state for protection, and was instrumental in the passing of the massive Central Arizona Project, bringing Colorado River water to the interior of the state. Although he was regarded as a strong environmentalist, he was pragmatic enough to see the need to reconcile the environment and the economy. He supported the Central Arizona Project, criticized today for the urban sprawl it helped create, but he also worked tirelessly to lessen its environmental damage. *The Almanac of American Politics* called Udall "one of the leading and most productive Democratic politicians of his generation."

Urban Revitalization

DURING THE LATE NINETIES modern Phoenix, with a population of 1.2 million, became the sixth largest city in America. The state's population had grown to five million. The Phoenix metropolitan area, with 2.3 million people, has nearly 50 percent of the state's total population.

The Phoenix Civic Plaza.

Phoenix had become a major-league city in many ways. The downtown America West Arena opened in June 1992, home to the NBA's Phoenix Suns, the WNBA's Phoenix Mercury, the NHL's Phoenix Coyotes, and arena football's Arizona Rattlers.

The Phoenix Civic Plaza, built in the seventies, was increased in size in the eighties and renovated in 1995. Phoenix Sky Harbor International Airport, serving thirty million commercial passengers a year, had its latest addition in 1990, with the opening of the Barry Goldwater Terminal. The new Central Library opened in 1995. The following year saw the opening of the new Arizona Science Center. In 1997 the sixty-eight-year-old Orpheum Theater was renovated and reopened.

Most of the credit for the highly successful revitalization of downtown Phoenix goes to the Bank One Ballpark, otherwise known as BOB. It opened for business in the spring of 1998 with the inaugural season of the Arizona Diamondbacks, who began play in baseball's National League. Thousands of baseball fans flock to the downtown area for each of the Diamondbacks' eighty-one home games, and downtown businesses are thriving. The warehouse district south of the ball park is undergoing massive renovation and conversion into shops and living areas.

Sports observers used to say that professional baseball would never fly in Phoenix, that it wasn't a baseball town. During the hot summers, people who could afford to go to ball games would opt instead for a beach vacation to San Diego or the cool pines of Pinetop, Prescott, or Flagstaff. During the fifties the Triple-A Phoenix Giants did poorly at the ticket office despite the presence of players like future Hall-of-Famer Willie McCovey. Even when the team relocated to Scottsdale's beautiful, mist-cooled park, attendance was low. Thus far, that's not been the case with the new Arizona Diamondbacks. Playing in their air-conditioned, natural grass, retractable-roof ballpark, the team is currently one of Major League Baseball's attendance leaders.

The ballpark was the subject of much controversy in the early nineties because the Maricopa County Board of Supervisors voted in a sales tax to fund the project instead of putting the vote to the public. The public outcry cost the board chairman, Jim Bruner, his political career as voters vented their anger at him. Bruner's political star was rising rapidly at the time. He'd served admirably on the Scottsdale City Council and the county Board of Supervisors. He entered the race for Congress in 1994 and was defeated by John Shadegg. Bruner's position on the stadium tax angered voters and played a major role in his defeat. Bruner deserved much of the credit for the downtown revitalization, and it was ironic that many who criticized him for voting to impose the sales tax to build the stadium later took bows for that revitalization.

Politicians have learned from experience that putting public projects like freeways, Rio Salado, and Val Trans up to a public vote is risky. Opponents of any new tax always have an easier time marshaling their forces on election day. In the fall of 1998, voters in the east Valley had an opportunity to pass or reject a tax for the controversial Rio Salado Crossing. The $1.7 billion project would include a domed stadium for the Arizona Cardinals, surrounded by parks, hotels, retail space, and office projects. Connected to the stadium is a large convention center, totaling one million square feet.

Other municipal projects of importance in recent years were the downtown restorations of Flagstaff, Glendale, and Mill Avenue in Tempe. All are examples of how free enterprise can turn lemons into lemonade. Tempe native and longtime mayor Harry Mitchell was the driving force behind the Mill Avenue restoration, which is an excellent example of public and private enterprise working together to revitalize a downtown area.

Taming the Growth Monster

IN THE 1990S Arizonans began to take a hard look at the phenomenal growth in their state. For years new developments had been leapfrogging across the desert like a swarm of locusts, devouring everything in sight. The infrastructure was in dire straits.

The decade saw increasing conflicts between developers and environmentalists. Someone suggested replacing the cactus wren as state bird with the construction crane. One quipster summed it up by declaring a developer is one who wants to develop a piece of desert land, and an environmentalist is one who already lives there.

Citizens of Scottsdale put their money where their mouth is and moved to a higher plane when they voted to tax themselves in order to buy desert land in prime development areas for preservation and public use. In 1989 Tempe citizens did the same when they voted to tax themselves to develop their own Rio Salado Project. It was the culmination of twenty years of environmental land planning. The five-mile stretch includes a combination of business, residential, and recreational areas along the banks of the Salt River near Sun Devil Stadium.

A massive Rio Salado Project along the river was turned down by Phoenix voters in the eighties. In 1998 a new Rio Salado Project was introduced to restore the river to a more natural state. Water would be pumped from the water table beneath the river bed. Construction would restore five miles of the river in Tempe and Phoenix. The river would support native wildlife and plant life. It would also create much-needed flood control and would reenergize the river channel through Phoenix. New neighborhoods would be developed, along with shopping centers and parks with hiking, bicycle, and horse trails. This time the major funding would come from the federal government through the 1998 Water Resources Development Act. The project is scheduled to begin in the year 2000 and to be completed three years later.

In July 1998, after four years of struggle and in the face of a court-ordered shutdown, the Arizona Legislature voted in favor of Governor Jane Hull's "Students FIRST" equalization program, which would provide an estimated nearly $400 million in state funding to construct, equip, and maintain schools at state-established minimum standards. The new law was the result of a lawsuit filed in 1991 on behalf of poorer school districts. Under the law a centralized system will set minimum building and adequacy standards and provide money to construct schools to those standards. Districts would still be able to pass capital overrides to pay for extra projects or facilities not included in the basic plan.

Strengthening efforts to preserve the past, in 1990 the Arizona Legislature passed two new laws designed to protect human burials and associated items on both private and state lands. These laws provide guidelines for construction projects and other land uses.

Trouble in Paradise

TOURISM IS THE LEADING JOB-producing industry in the state, creating more than three hundred thousand jobs. Billions of tourist dollars are pumped into the economy annually. But there's trouble in paradise: One of Arizona's—and America's—most enduring treasures is in danger. Congressional budget cutbacks in the 1990s have created a serious dilemma for the crown jewel of the national parks, Grand Canyon National Park.

Visitation at the state's number-one tourist attraction continues to increase. Currently, some five million people visit annually. Parking is next to impossible, with 7,500 vehicles a day fighting for some 2,500 parking spaces. Long lines of cars choke off the roads, spewing poisonous emissions into the air. More than 20 percent of the visitors report traffic and overcrowding as their most-remembered experience. In short, the Grand Canyon is being loved to death. By the end of the next decade the projected number of visitors is expected to double to ten million. Congress either can't or won't help. Forty percent of the visitors to the Grand Canyon are foreign and can't vote.

The Grand Canyon is nature's grandest natural architectural masterpiece. It can't be improved. The problems are manmade, and they can be solved. The Park Service has spelled out a general management plan that calls for a "quality visitor experience" and relies on the establishment of a gateway community at the entrance to the South Rim. A proposed solution is Canyon Forest Village, a gateway community at the south entrance to the Canyon at Tusayan that would meet the needs of the existing 3,500 local residents and the growing number of visitors to the Grand Canyon. The plan would relocate nonessential facilities and services to outside the park and restore the Canyon to its natural state. Canyon Forest Village also proposes to create community services, including schools, places of worship, and police, fire, and medical facilities that are presently nonexistent in Tusayan. It would include retail shops, hotels, and restaurants to generate profits to subsidize housing, public services, sustainable development technology, and an environmental preservation trust that will support conservation efforts.

The plan has met stiff resistance from established local businesses in Tusayan. However, nine national environmental groups have joined forces in an unprecedented coalition to support Canyon Forest Village as the best approach for dealing with growth pressure at the Canyon. The outcome is still in question as this book goes to press.

It's important to remember that we are all merely caretakers on this planet. The Grand Canyon was here long before we came and will be around long after we're gone. We need to take care of it and pass it along for future generations to enjoy.

FUTURE HISTORIANS will call this America's Century. She was the arsenal for democracy through two world wars. She gave tens of thousands of her young in the cause of world peace. She was living proof that democracy does indeed work, and demonstrated that process to emerging nations of the world. Her citizens enjoyed the highest standard of living in the history of the world. She held the line against Communism until it crumbled in its own morass, proving that a free, capitalistic society, though not perfect, is better than anything else devised by mankind. Through contributions to science, medicine, and technology, America has made the world a better place.

Futurists can't predict for certain where America will be a century from now. Evaluating a nation's niche in the grand scheme of history can only come from the wisdom of retrospect. Whether we did the right thing will have to be left for others to decide. We hope that in the year 2099, another writer will exam the events of the twenty-first century in the state and the nation and chronicle even greater achievements toward the freedom and glory of mankind.

In Arizona, one thing about the future is certain: The state will continue to have hot weather in the summer followed by cooler weather by late October, and cattle ranchers will complain it doesn't rain like it used to.

BIBLIOGRAPHY

BOOKS

America in the 20th Century, vols 1–10. New York: Marshal Cavandish. 1995.

Chronicle of the 20th Century. Liberty, MO: JL International Publishing. 1987.

Goldwater, Barry, with Jack Casserly. *Goldwater.* New York: Doubleday & Company. 1988.

Luckingham, Brad. *The Urban Southwest: A Profile History of Albuquerque, El Paso, Phoenix, and Tucson.* El Paso: Texas Western Press. 1982.

Mason, Herbert M. *The Great Pursuit.* New York: Random House. 1970.

Shadegg, Stephen C. *Arizona Politics.* Tempe: Arizona State University. 1986.

This Fabulous Century, vols 1–7. New York: Time-Life Books. 1970.

Trimble, Marshall. *Arizona: A Panoramic History of a Frontier State.* New York: Doubleday & Co. 1977.

————. *A Roadside History of Arizona.* Missoula: Mountain Press. 1986.

————. *Arizona: A Cavalcade of History.* Tucson: Treasure Chest Publications. 1989.

Wagoner, J. J. *Arizona's Heritage.* Salt Lake City: Peregrine Smith. 1977.

Wyllys, Rufus K. *Arizona: The History of a Frontier State.* Phoenix: Hobson and Herr. 1950.

NEWSPAPERS

"Arizona: A Rising Star, 1912–1987." *The Arizona Republic.* Sunday, February 15, 1987.

"Centennial." Special edition of *The Arizona Republic,* May 20, 1990.

INDEX

ABOUT THE AUTHOR

MARSHALL TRIMBLE grew up in the small town of Ash Fork, Arizona, a small cattle-shipping and railroad community on the Santa Fe mainline, and believes his small-town roots are responsible for the homespun humor of his stories and books. Inspired by a Kingston Trio concert, he began his career as a folk singer during the 1960s. Trimble has appeared on ABC's *Good Morning America* and CBS' *This Morning.* He has opened for major acts performing in the Phoenix area, including Waylon Jennings, Jerry Lee Lewis, and the Oak Ridge Boys.

Considered the dean of Arizona historians, Trimble is the author of more than a dozen books, and his stories and cowboy poems have appeared in such magazines as *Arizona Highways, Western Horseman,* and *The American Cowboy.* He's taught Arizona and Western history at the college level for twenty-five years. An avid outdoorsman, Trimble has seen most of Arizona's spectacular country from the back of a horse.